Gertrude Stein
and Richard Wright

Gertrude Stein
and Richard Wright

The Poetics and Politics of
MODERNISM

PS 3537
. T323
Z913
1998

1 00 99 98 4 3 2 1

The paper in this book meets the guidelines for permanence
and durability of the Committee on Production Guidelines for Book
Longevity of the Council on Library Resources.

Library of Congress Cataloging-in-Publication Data

Weiss, M. Lynn.
    Gertrude Stein and Richard Wright : the poetics and politics of
modernism / M. Lynn Weiss.
        p.   cm.
    Includes bibliographical references and index.
    ISBN 1-57806-100-8 (cloth : alk. paper)
    1. Stein, Gertrude, 1874–1946—Criticism and interpretation.
    2. Politics and literature—United States—History—20th century.
    3. Women and literature—United States—History—20th century.
    4. Wright, Richard, 1908–1960—Criticism and interpretation.
    5. American literature—20th century—History and criticism.
    6. Stein, Gertrude, 1874–1946—Friends and associates.   7. Wright,
Richard, 1908–1960—Friends and associates.   8. Afro-Americans—
Intellectual life—20th century.   9. Authors, American—20th
century—Biography.   10. Americans—France—History—20th century.
    11. Modernism (Literature)—United States.   12. Group identity in
literature.   13. Minorities in literature.   14. Poetics.   I. Title.
PS3537.T323Z913   1998
818'.5209—DC21   98-7786
                                                                          CIP

British Library Cataloging-in-Publication data available

for Rutha
first, last and always

Contents

Acknowledgments

Over the years, I have benefited from the intelligent, sensitive criticism and encouragement of many people. It is difficult to exaggerate the importance of their contributions to my work, and harder still to express my gratitude to them. Gerald Early read the manuscript and shepherded it and me over shaky ground. Michel Fabre read and advised on the Wright sections of the study. Rick Griffiths, a friend indeed, read, edited, added, posed nagging questions, and offered fresh insights. Michael North's work and criticism forced me to write a more rigorous version of the study. Julia Wright commented on and greatly improved the sections on her father's work. Many thanks to Carla Cappetti, Eddy Harris, Josef Jařab, and Eric Sundquist for wise instruction along the way.

I have been blessed with family and friends, all compassionate, smart, and very funny people, whose love and care helped me to write this book. A mahalo nui loa to Rutha, Mimi, George, Bonnie, Mark, Michael, Julie, Jenny, Larry, Nicolas, and Alex. I am very grateful to Funso Afolyan; Edna Arbuckle; Stephanie Borns-Weil; Laurie Fleischman; Valerie Géraud; Shafi Goldwasser; Janice Grossman; Francesca, Gordon, and Carlotta Lepingwell; Erin Mackie; Vicki Missien; Lisa Wenska Phee; Michèle Valencia; and Rafia Zafar.

For one year, this work was supported by a postdoctoral fellowship in Paris through the Centre Régional des Œuvres Universitaires et Scolaires. In addition, I would like to thank the librarians at the

Yale Collection of American Literature, Beinecke Rare Book and Manuscript Library at Yale University and at the Schomburg Center for Research in Black Culture; special thanks to Madame Mesnard at the Institut Mémoires de l'Édition Contemporaine in Paris. I am especially grateful to Ellen Wright for permission to quote from Richard Wright's unpublished work. Many thanks to Dorothy Negri in the Department of English and especially to Raye Riggins and Adele Tuchler in the Program for African and Afro-American Studies at Washington University.

This study came to fruition thanks to the wisdom, guidance, and generosity of Werner Sollors, my teacher and my friend.

Preface

If you wish to know who I am,
If you wish me to teach you what I know,
Cease for the while to be what you are
And forget what you know.

Tierno Bokar, the sage of Bandiagara

This study began as an exploration of expatriation through the works of Gertrude Stein and Richard Wright. Initially I chose these two because unlike many American expatriate artists, Stein and Wright remained in exile until their deaths. (They are buried a short walk from each other at Père Lachaise). Additionally, Stein, a Jewish lesbian, and Wright, an African-American, had complex if not agonized relationships to America and to an American identity. And finally, each writer's influence on American literature has been enormously important. Indeed at the close of the twentieth century, it is difficult to imagine American literature without *Three Lives* and *The Making of Americans* or *Black Boy* and *Native Son*. Among the most important things I would learn from my early research were the ways in which expatriation enabled these social, and in Stein's case literary, outcasts to be Americans in ways that were inaccessible to them back home. As it happened, the expatriation angle became an introduction to their insights on the relationship between the poetics of high modernism and its political implications for American life and art.

Moreover, the Stein/Wright friendship became an eloquent illustration of these insights.

Richard Wright made it difficult for his critics to ignore Stein's place in his biography. He had always publicly acknowledged his debt to Gertrude Stein; on numerous occasions and in many texts, he incorporated her into his narratives. More important she became a part of the narrative of his journey from rookie writer to literary star. But when I began this study, I did not know that Gertrude Stein read *Uncle Tom's Children, Black Boy* and *Native Son*. Most students of Gertrude Stein know that she read vociferously; but in the case of Richard Wright, there was something more. She was deeply interested in both the art and the subject matter of his work. More immediately this interest grew out of her experience of World War II, during which she and Alice B. Toklas spent four years in rural villages in eastern France. When the war was finally over, she returned to Paris to contemplate the role of racism in the making of America.

Recently, a senior scholar reported the following anecdote to me. In the early 1960s he had visited Mrs. William Aspenwell Bradley in Paris. After the war, Mrs. Bradley recalled, Gertrude Stein had sought her help in securing a visa for Richard Wright to visit Paris: "I've got to help him, you see, we are both members of minority groups." The spirit of this story is confirmed in a number of instances, in her work and in her role as godmother to the American servicemen stationed in Paris and witness to a devastated Europe. Richard Wright's work forced Stein to realize the social implications of her radical poetics. Without denying or diminishing the differences in gender, race, class, and sexual identity between them, it is possible, indeed inevitable, to see the striking parallels and overlapping concerns in their work.

In this study I consider texts with which the reader may not be familiar; to appreciate the implications of the Stein/Wright relationship for our literature and literary history we need to move beyond the canonical texts. Even though critics continue to evaluate his work in strictly literary terms, it is clear that to appreciate Richard Wright's legacy fully, we need to go beyond those boundaries. As Thornton Wilder wrote in an evaluation of Stein's *Four in America,*

"I think it can be said that the fundamental preoccupation of Miss Stein's life was not the work of art but the shaping of a theory of knowledge, a theory of time and a theory of the passions." With this in mind, if we move the discussion of their work from, in Salman Rushdie's memorable phrase, the "little room of literature" to the busy crossroads of cultural history, Gertrude Stein and Richard Wright become visible and audible philosophers of modernity whose meditations on the self, society, race, poetics, and politics are among the most subtle we have.

Two Lives:
Modernism and the Stein/Wright Connection

I do not think there has been anything done like it [Wright's Uncle Tom's Children] *since I wrote* Three Lives.

Gertrude Stein

The relationship between Gertrude Stein and Richard Wright is generally noted, but its implications are rarely explored. In the context of American literary history where Stein's friendships with Ernest Hemingway and Thornton Wilder or Wright's with James Baldwin and Ralph Ellison are central, the invisibility of the Stein/Wright relationship is suggestive. In most expatriate studies Stein and Wright are rarely considered in the same book, a reluctance perhaps to cross boundaries created by the critical practice of feminist, African-American, and ethnic studies. Such studies have made important contributions to American literary history, but their Linnaean impulse can obscure significant features of a writer's life and work. Richard Wright's work grew out of his experience as a black man from Mississippi who began his apprenticeship in Chicago; but as a thinker and a writer, he took lessons from Americans (such as Gertrude Stein) and Europeans, men and women on both sides of the color line. Similarly Gertrude Stein's *Three Lives* owes as much to black Baltimore and immigrant narratives as it does to Paul Cézanne, William James, or Gustave Flaubert. Our blindness to the Stein/Wright relationship and its implications for American literary history is related to the perception that these writers have very little in common.

Indeed Gertrude Stein and Richard Wright occupy opposite ends of the American spectrum. Stein was a white woman from the upper middle class, a graduate of Radcliffe College, who also completed four years of medical school at Johns Hopkins. Raised in a nonobservant Jewish household, Stein had lived in Vienna, Paris, Baltimore, and Oakland before she was ten years old. By 1908, the year Wright was born, Stein was thirty-four years old and had already completed *Three Lives* and was well into the composition of *The Making of Americans.*

Richard Wright, the son of a sharecropper, was born in rural Mississippi. The family's meager circumstances were made worse by the father's desertion and the mother's chronic illness. From a very early age, Wright worked at odd jobs and, because of his mother's frail health, his early schooling was marked by constant interruption; his formal education ended after the eighth grade. And although resistant to religious teachings, Wright was raised with the orthodoxy of his Seventh-Day Adventist grandmother.

These biographical differences between Gertrude Stein and Richard Wright are further demonstrated through a comparison of their work. Stein's radical experiments with language, best illustrated in *Three Lives, The Making of Americans,* and *Tender Buttons,* share little in common with Wright's *Uncle Tom's Children, Native Son,* or *Black Boy.* Apart from featuring an African-American community in "Melanctha," Stein's work is little concerned with such social realities, much less the social protest that drives Wright's fiction. Indeed these writers have come to represent two opposite tendencies in twentieth-century American literature; Stein is the avatar of art-for-art's-sake, while Wright is the politically conscious artiste engagé. Given such differences, the two should not have even liked each other.

Quite the opposite was true. Despite the silence that surrounds this friendship, both writers were very public in their mutual praise. In a 1945 article for the *New York Times Magazine,* Stein wrote, "when one Negro can write as Richard Wright does, writing as a

Negro about Negroes writes not as a Negro but as a man, well the minute that happens, the relation between the white and the Negro is no longer a difference of races but a minority question and ends . . . in persecution. That is the trouble, when people have equality there can be differences but no persecution" ("New Hope" 15, 38). When asked about her relationship with Wright during a 1946 interview, Stein reiterated her praise: "he has a great mastery of the English language and . . . to my mind, he has succeeded in doing the most creative work . . . done in many a year" (Haas 31–32). Stein concluded this interview by paying Wright the highest compliment: she compared his work to her own. Stein's enthusiasm for Wright's work prompted her to befriend him as well. In addition to their lively correspondence, Gertrude Stein played an important role in his first visit to France. When the U.S. State Department refused to grant him a passport, she helped obtain an invitation for him from the French government.

In her last two letters to Carl Van Vechten, Stein expressed some reservation in her estimation of Richard Wright. On June 12, 1946, she wrote, "he interests me immensely, he is strange, I have a lot of theories about him and sometime when it all gets straightened out I'll tell you . . . he has made quite clear to me the whole question of the Negro problem, the black white the white black, are they white or are they black . . . in his particular case it is very interesting, more so than in any of the others I have ever met" (Burns, *Letters of Stein and Van Vechten* 823, 827). In her next letter dated June 27, 1946, she does not commit herself any further except to say that there is a strange "materialism" about him that was not "Negro." The context does not clarify her meaning. She does seem a bit jealous of the attention Wright was getting from the French, which was very much in character, but she never retracted or qualified her praise of Wright's work.

Richard Wright's admiration for Gertrude Stein is equally well documented. It began when he read *Three Lives* in the early 1930s. Wright was in Chicago by this time and recalls having read an unflattering review of Stein's work. Stein's work was in the papers because she was on a lecture tour of the United States between the fall of 1934 and the spring of 1935. She gave a two-week seminar at the University of Chicago in the spring of 1935. Wright's published praise of Stein includes the piece, "Why I Chose Melanctha" and reviews of Stein's *Wars I Have Seen* and *Brewsie and Willie.* In the unpublished essay, "Memories of my Grandmother," Wright explores more fully Stein's influence on his thinking. In *American Hunger,* Wright cites Stein's influence on his early attempts to write, and in *Lawd Today!,* a novel attentive to the experimental prose and poetry of high modernism, one of the characters compares Stein's "rose is a rose is a rose" to a Cab Calloway scat. More privately, in an October 1945 letter to Stein in which he had enclosed a copy of *Black Metropolis,* Wright indicated where her essay "What Are Masterpieces" had influenced his introduction to that study. In January 1945, Wright wrote in his journal, "Am reading Stein's *Narration* and find it fascinating. . . . How odd that this woman who is distrusted by everyone can remind me of the most basic things in my life. . . . Yes, she's got something, but I'd say that one could live and write like that only if one lived in Paris or in some out of the way spot where one could claim one's own soul" (Journal, Jan. 1945). Indeed Wright admired the way Stein had, after years of expatriation, remained an original American voice.

In spite of the obvious and important differences in education, economic backgrounds, race, religion, and gender, Gertrude Stein and Richard Wright shared a similar intellectual landscape: they began their careers as marginals within already marginalized communities; their commitment to writing and their desire to live peacefully in unorthodox marriages led to permanent self-exile. The circumstances that led each writer to live abroad were qualitatively different, but both needed a distant haven. Even though the roads they traveled were not at all the same, Paris guaranteed a certain social and aesthetic freedom for both Stein and Wright. Stein left the United States, in part, to recover from a broken heart and a failed career in medicine. Paris offered a haven from the pressures and constraints of a highly educated woman struggling to come to terms with the heresy of her sexuality. The financial and moral support of her brothers, already in Paris, made the transition easier.

When Wright came to Paris in 1946, he was at the height of his career. In a letter to Stein dated May 27, 1945, he gleefully reported that *Black Boy* had sold 450,000 copies in eleven weeks. Despite the fame and fortune, which enabled him to purchase a home for his mother in Chicago and for his family in Greenwich Village, Wright was unable to escape the daily insults of his deeply racist native land: he was served salted coffee in neighborhood cafes when accompanied by his wife; neighborhood youths shouted racial epithets as he walked to and from home; his daughter was refused access to a toilet (Fabre, *Unfinished* 312). Wright knew that, in 1947, were he and Gertrude Stein to meet for coffee at a lunch counter in Mississippi it would provoke violence. Wright needed the refuge of a foreign land if he were to continue to write. Each writer made only one trip back to the United States in all their years of expatriation; Stein spent forty-three years abroad and Richard Wright spent thirteen. Unlike most expatriate writers, Stein and Wright died and are buried in Paris. And despite the decades away from their native land and the critique this absence implies, both writers insisted upon their American identity; indeed expatriation enabled them to be Americans in ways inaccessible to them back home.

During their separate apprenticeships, both writers had to struggle against a domineering influence upon which they were dependent. Gertrude Stein's unusually close relationship to her brother Leo began to fracture when she persisted in her literary experimentation. Although Stein was reticent on this subject, Leo's assessment of his sister as "basically stupid" supports her telegraphic account of the relationship in *The Autobiography*; Leo ridiculed her every effort. In his autobiography, Leo Stein expressed his objections to both Picasso's cubism and his sister's writing: "Both he and Gertrude are using their intellects, which they ain't got, to do what would need the finest critical tact, which they ain't got either, and they are in my belief turning out the most Godalmighty rubbish that is to be found" (53).

Richard Wright's battle to become a writer began in childhood. *Black Boy-American Hunger* chronicles many of these conflicts, and although Wright did exaggerate some of the details, one can easily imagine the ways a black boy from rural Mississippi in the early decades of this century would have been discouraged from a career as a writer. Among the conflicts Wright includes are his grand-mother's refusal to let him read anything but books approved by her church; the racism of the white South and black complicity when the school principal gives Richard the speech he is to read for com-mencement in lieu of the one he had written; the librarians who would not have let him borrow books, much less anything by Mencken. To the problem of race, add class; Richard Wright did not come from the middle-class milieu of W. E. B. Du Bois or James Weldon Johnson. Finally Wright includes the American Communist Party's censure for his failing to toe the line.

Wright's conflict with the American Communist Party should not be underestimated. Although he was bright and ambitious, his dream of becoming a writer would have been impossible in the con-text of the Great Depression without the help of party affiliates such as the John Reed Club or the *Daily Worker.* Richard Wright did not have the intellectual or financial support that such writers as Zora Neale Hurston, Langston Hughes, and Ralph Ellison acquired through their college experiences. Instead the Chicago branch of the John Reed Club and later the New York office of the *Daily Worker* provided cultural, intellectual, and financial support, and ultimately through the journals *Left Front* and *New Masses,* the party published Wright's early work. For a number of years Richard Wright flour-ished in that milieu. He became the John Reed Club's executive secretary and organized a lecture series that brought several pro-gressive professors from the University of Chicago to lecture. Wright met Professor Louis Wirth through his wife Mary Wirth because she was the Wright family's social worker. But only in his capacity as the club's secretary would Wright have been able to encounter scholars such as Melville Herskovits, John Strachey, and Robert Morss Lovett (Fabre, *Unfinished* 100–130). The break was inevitable; the party expected Wright to produce party-line literature and to recog-nize that party politics were more important than writing. The most important event leading to this break turned on the issue of race. Wright objected to the party's decision to withhold support from any effort to combat government discrimination in the courts in the guise of wartime solidarity. Wright expressed much of his frustration with the party in "I Tried to Be a Communist" and in *American Hunger*.

Each writer fought a war on two fronts: where the uncertainty of her/his literary ambitions lived, and in the daily struggle to be free from the support that had once been vital. These battles were inevitable and prolonged. Even though Stein's writing and the arrival of Alice Toklas had begun to separate them as early as 1908, Leo Stein did not leave 27 rue de Fleurus until 1913. And although Richard Wright knew that he would have to leave the party as early as 1935, he did not officially sever his ties until 1942 (Fabre, *Unfinished* 207–46). There was a finality to these breaks; Stein never again spoke to Leo after their separation nor did Wright ever forgive the American Communist Party.

Our efforts to appreciate the affinities between Gertrude Stein and Richard Wright are further frustrated by apparently irreconcilable differences between the modernisms of black and white American writers. Houston Baker's *Modernism and the Harlem Renaissance* and Paul Gilroy's *Small Acts: Thoughts on the Politics of Black Cultures* speak to the important differences in the black writer's use of modernism. For Houston Baker any cultural form that is "designated 'modernist' for Afro-America is also, and by dint of adequate historical accounts, always, co-extensively labeled popular, economic and liberating" (101). Unlike white writers, the African-American writer's modernist "anxiety" is produced by the daunting task of having to use "audible extant forms" to move beyond the legacy of slavery (101). Developing this point further, Gilroy argues that it is possible to reconcile the "aesthetics of personalism and the matching politics of radical individualism" and that this reconciliation is best expressed by the idea of a "populist modernism," developed by Werner Sollors to describe the work of Leroi Jones/Amiri Baraka. This apparent oxymoron acknowledges black writers' roles as creators and critics of modernism who are also aware of their obligations to the history of the black Atlantic in the making of modernity. Gilroy defines populist modernism in these terms:

This distinctive aesthetic and ethico-political approach requires a special gloss on terms like reason, justice, freedom, and "communicative ethics." It starts from the recognition of the African diaspora's peculiar position as "step-children" of the West and of the extent to which our imaginations are conditioned by an enduring proximity to regimes of racial terror. It seeks deliberately to exploit the distinctive quality of perception that Du Bois identified long ago as "double consciousness." Whether this is viewed as an effect of oppression or a unique moral burden, it is premised on some sense of black cultures . . . as counter-cultures of modernity forged in the quintessentially modern condition of racial slavery. (*Small Acts* 103)

In the manifesto, "Blueprint for Negro Writing," Richard Wright emphasizes these points. African-American writers had to create with an awareness of the history of slavery and racial terror; "Negro writers must have in their consciousness the foreshortened picture of the *whole,* nourishing culture from which they were torn in Africa, of the long, complex . . . struggle to regain in some form and under alien conditions of life a *whole* again" (47). Moreover, to preserve the creative perspective, black writers had to connect this history to a global history, to see the lives of African Americans in New York and Chicago with the awareness that "one sixth of the earth's surface belongs to the working class" (46). Wright's position argues for a modernism that draws on both African-American folk traditions and the modernist discursive strategies of Stein, Proust, and Hemingway.

Richard Wright's first novel, *Lawd Today!,* is an early example of a populist modernism. Published posthumously in 1960, *Lawd Today!* makes explicit references to Stein, Dos Passos, and Joyce. The story takes place on a single day, February 12, a holiday celebrating the birth of Abraham Lincoln. The narrative is continually interrupted by blaring newspaper headlines, advertisements, and radio. In this example, Jake, the protagonist is reading the morning paper:

He stirred his cup and read again.
EINSTEIN SAYS SPACE BENDS
"Humph! Now this is what I call crazy! Yes, siree, just plumb crazy!

This guy takes the prize. What in hell do he know about space bending." (32)

When the discussion turns to the relative sanity of white people, one of the characters cites Stein's "rose is a rose is a rose" as proof of their insanity, but another compares this phrase to jazz scats (174). Linking this most famous of Stein's reiterations to a jazz scat, Wright suggests that such artists might drink from the same well. Even as it playfully evokes modernist literary strategies, *Lawd Today!* never veers from its serious subject; black life in America. The African-American writer's need for a populist modernism is argued again in Wright's brilliant story "The Man Who Lived Underground."

Richard Wright's sense of the relationship between Calloway's scat jazz and the poetics of highly experimental formalism of Stein, Joyce, or the surrealists turns on the idea that "forced exclusion from this conventional world has led black Americans to: the production of an obliqueness of vision, a different way of looking at the world, of conceiving and feeling it" (Miller 82). The odd and disturbing poetics of high modernism began in the writer's sense of uncertainty and alienation. And while the sense of standing on shaky ground may have been new to white writers (although perhaps to a lesser degree for Joyce and Stein than for Eliot and Pound), it was familiar terrain for black writers. Although Wright could agree with the disruptive dimension of modernist poetics, unless these were grounded in a historical consciousness the road would lead to Freddy Daniels's cave.

"The Man Who Lived Underground" was written in 1942 in the important interval between *Native Son* and *Black Boy*. The story is familiar: Freddy Daniels is falsely accused of murdering a white woman. The police beat him until he signs a confession, but remarkably he escapes, taking refuge in the sewer. Once underground, the narrative moves from the naturalist world of *Native Son* to an eerily disturbing other world; indeed it is *le monde à l'envers*. As Eugene Miller has noted, the composition of this piece coincided with Wright's reading Freudian dream theory and surrealism. The forced exclusion from life and the alienation this produces in Freddy is evoked through the antirational strategies of surrealism: "the dead world of sunshine" and "obscene sunshine," "the dark sunshine aboveground," and the placement of familiar objects out of context. A furtive interloper, Freddy steals gems, currency, tools, a radio, and a typewriter from the aboveground. Here too the surrealist aesthetic is invoked: Freddy uses hundred-dollar bills to paper the walls of his cave and then nails up wristwatches and a meat cleaver. Diamonds become encrusted in the dirt of the cave's floor and remind Freddy of the starry night sky.

Carla Cappetti has argued persuasively that "The Man Who Lived Underground" criticizes the hermetically sealed universe of the radically experimental formalism of the surrealists, including the more obscure work of Gertrude Stein. "The Man Who Lived Underground" illustrates the limits of experimental formalism for Richard Wright. The extent to which the "complex simplicity" of black American life could be expressed through such radical formalism was limited by its narrow focus on the subjective (Cappetti, *"Black Boy"*). (Besides which, as Wright knew so well, jazz was black America's radical formalism.) In a 1938 interview for *Columbia University Writers Club Bulletin,* Wright makes this point: "All of us young writers were influenced by Hemingway . . . We liked the simple, direct way in which he wrote, but a great many of us wanted to write about social problems . . . Hemingway's style is so concentrated upon naturalistic detail that there is no room for social `comment" (Fabre, *Richard Wright* 71). Which is not to argue that Richard Wright sacrificed aesthetics for the social and political commitment. Indeed the enduring power of his work is its ability to use these forms, as Houston Baker suggests, "in ways that move clearly up, masterfully and resoundingly away from slavery" (101). More important, Richard Wright did not so much learn from white modernists as he recognized in their poetics the sense of alienation and estrangement with which he and most black Americans were quite familiar.

Eugene Miller makes a solid case for the influence of the formally radical modernists during Wright's apprenticeship. Miller's discussion includes passages from an unpublished story, "Tarbaby's

Dawn," which resonates with the language of "Melanctha." Note this striking example: "Gradually he began to see and feel it all and he felt her helping him to feel her and then he had her, feeling him and her coming to a dark red point of hotness and blazing red and red and red" (63). Even though Wright did not employ these formal strategies in his canonical work, Stein's prose helped him to see literary style as not "merely . . . external and decorative but as interior and integral . . . the form chosen to make the work perceivable" (66). Wright ultimately chose the narrative strategies of naturalism and realism because, as Cappetti argues, he needed forms that would best convey the stories of black American life he hoped to tell. In Emile Zola's novels of the desperately poor in pitiless urban squalor, *Nana* and *L'Assommoir,* Wright found a parallel to the story of Chicago's black ghetto. Recall too that the earliest sociological studies depended on many Zola-inspired narratives, or "life stories." In the United States, this was the practice of the Chicago School—to keep theory about human migration and social change grounded in human experience (20–31). Naturalism, realism, and the highly formal modernism of Joyce and Stein share a sense of the displacement of a religious for a secular worldview, of alienation, and a focus on human consciousness, perception, and cognition. Gertrude Stein and Richard Wright were influenced by the social sciences engaged in the study of human consciousness in a strange new world.

David Hollinger rightly challenges the conventional notion of literary modernism as being in opposition to modern science. Hollinger notes that the term "modernism" is most closely associated with early twentieth-century literature, which is characterized by an "anti-rational, alienated and experimental style." But this "dominant reading of modernism as anti-rational, experimental and alienated" obscures the rational and scientific aspect of modernity and what we think of as the Modern (38). We need not deny the term "modernism" to this literary and artistic movement, but we need to recall that it represents one of many responses to modernity. Another, as important, response is that of the scientist; we are as much the children of Charles Darwin as of William Butler Yeats. One of the features of "modernism" for the artist as well as for the scientist is the celebration of the "cognitive capability of human beings." Indeed, "many of the careers we normally take to be major episodes in the intellectual history of the last century were responsive to both" (42–45). This certainly describes Gertrude Stein and Richard Wright and further illuminates their intellectual and temperamental affinities.

Intellectually, Stein and Wright were influenced by the new social sciences of psychology and sociology. Both disciplines articulate two important theories associated with modernism that were fundamental to their work: the focus on human consciousness informed by new scientific theories of the self and the alienation of the self in the modern urban setting. For Gertrude Stein there was nothing more important than "the relationship of the self to the self." In the early decades of this century, sociology offered a persuasive paradigm for understanding the major upheavals in American society provoked by mass immigration from Europe as well as the Great Migration of black Americans from the rural South to northern cities. Richard Wright's encounter with the theories of Louis Wirth and Robert Park enabled him to see the African-American experience in the context of a global transformation that is the hallmark of modernity. In this context, an individual life could not be adequately understood outside his/her conflict with community both large and small.

At Harvard between 1894 and 1896, Gertrude Stein was present at the beginning of an entirely new discipline in American higher education: William James's courses in psychology. Stein's scientific training, first as an undergraduate at Harvard and later as a medical student, made her extremely attentive to states of consciousness as revealed through speech. Her insights for narrative, that is, repetition and the continuous present, are grounded in this scientific training. Stein's first publication, "Normal Motor Automatism" (*Psychological Review*, 1896), which she coauthored with Leon Solomons, reported the results of an experiment to measure responses to fatigue. Even after her career in medical school came to an end, Stein spent another semester in the laboratory doing brain research (Bridgman 37). This background, particularly Jamesian psychology, enabled Stein to think and to write with a new kind of subjectivity.

The idea that gave impetus to *The Making of Americans,* to "describe the bottom nature of everyone who was ever living," had its origins in her scientific background. But just as important, another of Stein's objectives in writing *The Making of Americans* was to show "the old world in the new or more exactly the new world all made out of the old." In her mind, psychology that revealed the subject in new ways was linked to the prototypical American form. All that is familiar in the immigrant family narrative of assimilation is sabotaged by the novel's form, which creates a modernist aesthetic as it expresses the modernity of the American experience. For Gertrude Stein, the narrative of her American experience runs aground on available forms. Or as Pricilla Wald has argued, "Stein's telling differs from conventional immigrant narratives because she wants to tell the story of that telling-of the difference between what the narrator *means* to tell and of what she can actually tell" (257). All of Stein's formal innovations worked (borrowing an expression from jazz) to "worry," to question, the relationship between sign and signified, noun and referent, lived experience and its representation. This is echoed in the title, where process is privileged over fixity. Process, that which is evolving and therefore indeterminate was, for Stein, key to her own identity as an artist and an American. Stein's modernism came out of her scientific training and the dialectic of her experience as both an American and, like Richard Wright, an outsider. With the exception of Henry James, no writer at the turn of the century illustrates more vividly the artist's struggle to make cognitive process part of the artistic production than does Gertrude Stein. *Three Lives* (1906), *The Making of Americans* (1911), and *Tender Buttons* (1914) are the founding texts of American literary modernism.

In *Writing Chicago: Modernism, Ethnography, and the Novel,* Carla Cappetti has demonstrated the extent to which Richard Wright's thinking was influenced by the Chicago School of Sociology. Much of Wright's prose, fiction and nonfiction, would ultimately be shaped by the idea of the Marginal Man, the peasant who migrates from the rural Past to the urban Now. It is the paradigm developed by Robert Park and the Chicago School of Sociology. Wright accounts for the centrality of this paradigm to his work in his introduction to St. Clair Drake and Horace Cayton's *Black Metropolis: A Study of Negro Life in a Northern City:* "I did not know what my story was, and it was not until I stumbled upon science that I discovered some of the meanings of the environment that battered and taunted me . . . The huge mountains of fact piled up by the Department of Sociology at the University of Chicago gave me my first concrete vision of the forces that molded the urban Negro's body and soul" (Drake and Cayton 18–19). The sociological model kept Wright's modernist perspective grounded in the world he was committed to making visible.

Richard Wright appropriated two concepts from Robert Park's essay "Human Migration and the Marginal Man" that catalyzed his thinking and writing about the African-American experience, including his own. In this essay, Park argues that social change comes out of catastrophe and from that social chaos (the Great Migration from the South to the northern urban centers, or the vast influx of immigrants from eastern Europe) there emerges a new man (and woman) who culturally embodies both the old order and the new. He is "a man on the margin of two cultures." Marginal Man is freed from the "local bonds . . . from the culture of the tribe and folk . . . from the sacred order of tribal custom" (345–56). Louis Wirth focuses on a related problem: a sociological definition of the city. Wirth begins with a design that contrasts the rural (the world of kinship and unity, of emotional attachment) with the urban (the world of freedom, sophistication, and tolerance but also alienation, insecurity, and powerlessness). Park's Marginal Man lives on the bridge spanning these two worlds (60–83).

The Chicago School of Sociology provided Wright with a powerful model from which he created one of the century's most enduring metaphors: the marginal, alienated black boy. The structure of *Black Boy-American Hunger* owes much to the sociological model of conflict "between groups and individuals, community and society, tradition and modernity, nature time and clock time" (Cappetti, *Writing* 196). Wright also drew on the slave narrative and the portrait-of-the-artist genres to tell his story. But what made *Black Boy* more than another portrait of the artist or neo-slave narrative was his incorporation of the conflict around which both sociological theory and literary modernism, in the United States and Europe, had developed (196). Wright's genius lay in his ability to see that the black American experience was an extraordinarily rich instance of the conflict between tradition and modernity, between the individual and the community as the hallmark of modernity. Richard Wright's gift to world literature was to move the Other from the circumference to the center of modern life. To understand modernity, in all its complexity, white Americans had to come to terms with the black American; "the Negro" he argued, "is America's metaphor" (*White Man* 72). In most of his expatriate writing, Wright extended the discussion of what W. E. B. Du Bois referred to as the problem of the twentieth century beyond America's borders to include the entire world.

These new models of self and society enabled Gertrude Stein and Richard Wright to express substantively and stylistically their own complex alienation. The psychological and sociological paradigms contributed to and formalized each writer's psychological and emotional distance from his/her material. This distance enables what I call the modernist impulse to make visible the ways in which social forms (Jim Crow) and literary practices (syntax) are culturally determined and culturally relative. As such, Wright's metaphors and Stein's discursive strategies are important instances of cultural critique. Marianne DeKoven argues that Stein's encrypted narratives were in part a response to disturbing feelings about her sexuality but that "Stein did not merely stifle or deny her anger, her sense that she did not fit and that the deficiency was not hers but rather that of the structure which excluded her" (36).

In the unpublished essay "Memories of My Grandmother," Wright recalls an incident that captures the quality he most appreciated in the prose of Gertrude Stein. One summer day during the Loeb-Leopold trial, Wright's family had gathered on the porch to listen to an uncle read a newspaper account. Young Wright was struck by the fact that these men could speak several languages. He then announced to the elders, "I wish I could forget English for a few minutes, just so I could listen to it and hear how it sounds" (Journal 16). Years later, when Wright describes how Stein's *Three Lives* had enabled him to hear English as never before, that childhood wish is evoked; "I heard English as Negroes spoke it: . . . melodious, tolling, rough, infectious, subjective, laughing, cutting . . . Words which I'd know all of my life but . . . never really heard. . . . And not only the words, but the winding psychological patterns that lay back of them!" (Journal 19). Eugene Miller raises the point many critics and writers have observed over the years; Melanctha doesn't sound black, at least not by conventional/stereotypical standards, then or now. So what was it in "Melanctha" that so reminded him of Grandmother Wilson? In part Wright heard the repetitions that are intrinsic to the African-American folkloric tradition. And as important, Wright, "heard . . . not what Stein's characters were saying but rather Stein's attitude toward language. . . . she made him aware of a validity in language that was not in the scientific mode . . . but in its sensory qualities, as music or incantation" (Miller 72).

The meaning of the words or an odd syntax are less important than "the intonation of her voice, the rhythm of her simple, vivid sentences. . . . 'Melanctha' was written in such a manner that I could actually stand outside of the English language and hear it" (Journal 20). The ability to "stand outside of the English language" is key to the linguistic innovations of high modernism. Making it new meant in part making it strange.

In *The Dialect of Modernism*, Michael North's discussion of Malinowski's theory of language illuminates Wright's desire to stand outside of the English language. Malinowski's experiences as an anthropologist led him to conceive of language as that which enables "phatic communion." Meaning is secondary: "the primary function of language, all language, is not to convey meaning at all but to facilitate the social communion without which it has no existence" (46). (This is North's paraphrase of Bonislaw Malinowski, "The Problem of Meaning in Primitive Languages.") North argues for the centrality of this concept in the work of Joseph Conrad. For Conrad, who referred to "phatic communion" as solidarity, "the power of sound has always been greater than the power of sense" (47). This "solidarity" is inaccessible to the linguistic outsider; conversely, those within the magic circle are unaware of it. Through Stein's *Three Lives,* Wright becomes a linguistic outsider long enough to hear the "solidarity" of southern, rural, Christian, black America in his grandmother's voice. The implications are important; Wright could apperceive this solidarity only to the extent he already felt himself outside of it. The modernism of Richard Wright's work, its striking prescience and in-surgency, grew out of his being the insider who is simultaneously the outsider.

Richard Wright's reading of *Three Lives* influenced the way he would represent the African-American experience. In "Memories" he links the Conradian sense of the "solidarity" of language to the "surreal" quality of black American life that is characterized by *"psychological distance*—even when it deals with realistic subject matter" (Journal 20). For black Americans this distance is *"enforced severance . . .* through unemployment, oppression from the functional meaning of society" (20). The link between what Wright called his grandmother's "abstract" way of living in but not of the world be-cause of her religious beliefs and Stein's highly stylized prose is an emotional and psychological distance. It is that quality in Stein's work that he describes as being possible only "if one lived in Paris or in some out of the way spot where one could claim one's own soul." Wright and Stein did, in part, achieve that distance through expatriation. But expatriation simply completes and confirms the ex-isting psychological and perhaps spiritual alienation.

In *Paris France* and elsewhere Stein insisted on the artist's need for two countries. Especially in France, she was content to have been "left alone with my eyes and my english." But in "Melanctha" Stein had also achieved an emotional distance by locating the story of her own failed love affair in Baltimore's African-American community. North argues that Stein's assumption of an African-American per-sona also functioned as a kind of cultural expatriation and helped to further free her, psychologically and formally, from her bourgeois origins (59–76). Ironically, Stein's need for distance to narrate an episode of personal crisis prompted her to approximate an African-American idiom that would someday enable a striving young black writer to embrace, from a distance, a troubled relationship of his own. "Melanctha" as much as Mencken or the Chicago School of Sociology helped Richard Wright to find his voice.

Unlike T. S. Eliot or Ezra Pound, Stein appropriated a black voice as much from an identification with the blues of black folk, particularly as a Jew and a lesbian, as from its function as a distancing strategy. Gertrude Stein's interest in Richard Wright and his work grew out of her attentiveness to the African-American presence and experience in America. In a 1945 interview for the *Baltimore Afro-American*, Gertrude Stein told journalist Vincent Tubbs, "I am interested in the cultural products of the world like Richard Wright's *Black Boy* which I think heralds an evolution from intellectual defensiveness to intellectual offensiveness." And toward the end of the interview Stein stated, "The things we have talked about today we did not talk about twenty five years ago and what you say is interesting and I could see it in Wright's book which I think is really epochal because it means the colored race is no longer the white man's burden and is conversing himself about himself and magnificently too" (5). During the last months of her life, between April 1945 and July 1946, Gertrude Stein read, corresponded with, and finally met Richard Wright.

This period coincided with the euphoric end of World War II, and, given her experience of that war, it is not surprising that Stein would be impressed by *Black Boy* and its young author. Racist propaganda, aimed primarily at Jews, gypsies, and foreigners, had dominated the French media during the war. Rather than quit their adopted country, Stein and Toklas spent the period between 1939 and 1944 in two small rural villages in eastern France. Like the French majority, Stein had initially backed Philippe Pétain's Vichy government. Pétain's overwhelming popular support was owing to his astounding heroism in the decisive World War I battle of Verdun. Pétain's victory had encouraged Stein and Toklas to return to France, where between 1916 and 1918 they were volunteers with the

"American Fund for French Wounded." For their work, which involved driving supplies all over the south of France, Stein and Toklas were awarded le Médaille de la Reconnaissance Française in 1922 (Brinnin 220–31).

That Gertrude Stein actually translated 180 pages of the marshal's speeches and kept her friendship with Bernard Faÿ, an Americanist who became head of the Bibliothéque Nationale during the Vichy regime, continues to be troubling. It is unclear, as Edward Burns and Ulla Dydo note, why, once Pétain's anti-Semitic policies began to result in deportations, Stein continued to work on the speeches (401–21). Stein and Toklas were protected by Pétain through Faÿ, and perhaps this impaired her judgment. However much we must fault Stein and Toklas for their conservative politics, we are obligated to distinguish between conservative politics and Nazi collaboration. Stein and Toklas had seen the consequences of World War I, "when all the men were dead or badly wounded" (Van Vechten 633). In retrospect can one fault them or the French if they preferred a negotiated peace to another war? Should she have refused Faÿ's protection, whom she had known since 1926, of not just herself but her art collection in Paris? Might we be more forgiving had she, like Joyce, gone to Switzerland? It made more sense to stay in France; Stein and Toklas were well integrated into the small rural communities in Belley and Culoz and had spent every summer in that region for the previous twenty years. In addition, both women were in their mid- to late sixties during the war. It can be argued that Stein simply followed the example of her own government; the United States never severed its ties to the Vichy government either.

This history is further complicated by Stein's contributions, in 1942–43, to a monthly arts journal, *Confluences*. It was published in Lyons, as opposed to Paris, and enjoyed a certain amount of independence because of it. *Confluences'* critics complained that it published the work of "Jews, communists and pederasts." During that somber period, it was among few journals open to the increasingly numerous anti-Vichy writers. Stein's poem, "Ballade" appeared in the famous July 1942 edition in which Louis Aragon published

"Nymphée," a thinly disguised critique of the French and the Vichy government. For this offense, the publication of *Confluences* was suspended for two months. Stein's "Ballade" also takes up the idea of the necessity of resistance by the weaklings against the stronger bullies. In August 1943, René Tavernier, *Confluences*' editor wrote to inform Stein that her name appeared on the list "OTTO," those writers whose work could not be published in France. Stein's status as a Jewish writer earned her this distinction (Burns and Dydo 419–20). Having read Gertrude Stein's letters to René Tavernier at Institut Mémoires de l'Edition Contemporaine in Paris, I could not determine how she responded to this news; her correspondence with Tavernier, which had up to that point been fairly regular, stopped abruptly for one year.

After the war, Stein and Toklas went to Germany for *Life* magazine. The two women made a tour of the American army bases, and, along with a troop of American soldiers, they visited Hitler's mountain retreat in Berchtesgarten, Austria. There Stein and the soldiers had their photo taken on the terrace in mock Third Reich salute. During this tour, a black soldier approached Stein and recited her poetry, an incident that moved her. The Third Reich's racist ideology that had driven World War II, combined with its reflection in America's Jim Crow army, prompted Gertrude Stein to "meditate" on the race problem. In the *Life* article, Stein chastises Americans who must learn to appreciate the "Other" to learn to think for themselves, and she points to defeated Germany as an example of all that was wrong in the world. So explicit was her social criticism that the sergeant presented her with a card that read "to Gertie, another Radical" ("Off" 54–58). There is a photo that puts a finer point on Stein's own criticism of American racism; in it she is standing among a group of African-American soldiers in occupied Germany (Stendahl 248–49; the photo is the property of the Beinecke Library, Yale University). Stein's meditations on race and racism dominated her thinking until her death.

Stein had initially written to Wright to praise *Black Boy*, which she read after his favorable review of *Wars I Have Seen*. She also asked that he send copies of his other work that were still unavailable in postwar Paris. Wright happily complied and, in addition, sent her a copy of Dan Burly's *Handbook to Harlem Jive* and some of Father Divine's speeches. Stein plied Wright with questions about racism in America; Stein's interest in the subject had taken on new intensity. By July she was reading Gunnar Myrdal's landmark study, *An American Dilemma.* In a July 6, 1945, letter to Carl Van Vechten, she asked for any work by black educator Kelly Miller (Burns, *Letters of Stein and Van Vechten* 782–83). By August, Stein had received and read *Uncle Tom's Children* and wrote, "I'm mad about it, there is a tremendous mastery in the thing" (789). Vincent Tubbs interviewed Stein for the *Baltimore Afro-American* because she had made it publicly known that she wanted to talk to black servicemen. "This correspondent went to see Miss Stein because I believe anybody who wants to know colored people should be given the opportunity" (Tubbs 5). And in *Brewsie and Willie,* a novel that features American GIs, the black soldiers surpass the white soldiers in creativity and ambition.

In a 1993 essay on Gertrude Stein and Nella Larsen, Corinne Blackmer found it remarkable that, despite the shared concerns and masking strategies of "Melanctha" and *Passing,* there had been no comparative study of these texts. Blackmer suggests that this critical silence stemmed, in part, from the taboo surrounding lesbian fiction, and she notes, "that exclusive focus on one category of difference tends to inhibit analysis of how overlapping differences operate in syncopation" (232). This is not to argue that the race, gender, class, and education differences between them were unimportant. The experience as outsider shaped their lives and work, but neither Stein nor Wright could be bound by categories of race, gender, or class in life or art. I proceed with two premises in mind: I take seriously their friendship, however brief or mediated, and I assume that their overlapping differences make it possible to discuss their work together.

This study is divided into three parts, each of which discusses two works by Gertrude Stein and Richard Wright. These texts are related thematically; for example, Gertrude Stein's *Everybody's Autobiography* (1937) and Richard Wright's *Black Power* (1954) narrate the authors' journeys "home." I discuss Stein's *Lectures in America* (1934) in conjunction with Wright's collection of lectures *White Man, Listen!* (1956) and also consider Stein's *Paris France* (1940) with Wright's *Pagan Spain* (1954). I have chosen these texts not because they are representative (although "vintage" comes to mind) Stein and Wright but because they are not. That is, these texts are the thought pieces and meditations wherein we glimpse the minds at work. In these texts, the writers adopt different personae who can pose questions that the voices of *Tender Buttons* and *Native Son* could not, which is, in part, the point. Their own questions determined their destinies if not their destinations. They journeyed far, and these texts are part of the extraordinary map of this long neglected legacy.

In chapter 2, I examine how Gertrude Stein and Richard Wright use a foreign country to meditate on expatriation and their role as writers. The narratives reveal the way a foreign context confers the authority that odd folk like Gertrude Stein and Richard Wright need. Stein begins *Paris France* with this paradox: "America is my country and Paris is my hometown." This apparently simple memoir is an effort to come to terms with the central paradox of her life. Gertrude Stein had needed France to become the mother of twentieth-century American literature. One of the popular fictions about Richard Wright is that expatriation effectively ruined his work because it severed him from the source of his inspiration. *Pagan Spain*, which begins with instructions and a blessing from the dying Gertrude Stein, addresses this complaint and more. Even though Langston Hughes had an international reputation, Richard Wright was the first African American to share the world's stage with writers such as James Joyce and Albert Camus. And this role, what he would write about and why, moving him from the provinces to the center of post–World War II conflict, shares the spotlight with Wright's acknowledged goal of the narrative.

Wright went to Spain, as Stein advised, to "see the past, to see what the Western World is made of." He went to see the vestiges of an empire whose fortunes were built on the slave trade, and in this script Spain is Western imperialism as the origin of the modern world. Wright also went to Spain to revise the romantic and sentimental narratives of his compatriots. As he retraces the footsteps of Washington Irving and Ernest Hemingway, he corrects their Spanish narratives and challenges the Anglo-American version of American history. And as he revises these narratives, he writes himself into American literary history. Future versions of this history must include Wright's voice, Wright's version. Distance from America afforded Wright the luxury of being more than just another black writer of protest fiction. But Wright did more than determine the direction of his own career; he bore witness to the global revolution in politics, economics, and the arts that we call the postcolonial period. The four works of nonfiction published between 1954 and 1957 make explicit his commitment to the emerging nations of Africa and Asia and to keeping this new world order visible both in the United States and Europe.

In chapter 3, I consider the concepts of race and nation at the core of American identity through the homecoming narratives of *Everybody's Autobiography* and *Black Power*. In these texts each writer challenges again and again the adequacy of these categories to describe modern identity. In *Everybody's Autobiography,* Stein's narrative of the lecture tour that brought her back to the United States for the first and only time, she revises and repudiates at every turn the American obsession to define, control, and exclude the Other. This account fuses her radically experimental work with its rejection of formal authority to her Americanness that, as she defined it, cannot be defined. Originality in life and in art is related to having been raised on the margins of the nation that, because it is process, "did not really know what it was." In *Everybody's Autobiography,* nouns that announce essentialism such as "Jew," "woman," "Californian," and "lesbian" are refuted. Stein's chief criticism of America was its denial of process and its wholehearted investment in the meaningfulness of these categories. This is explicit in one of her most quoted quips, "What is the use of being a boy if you are going to grow up to be a man." Stein's homecoming was an occasion to worry the notion of a fixed identity the external expression of which is home.

Richard Wright's resistance to the definitiveness of race as a category is at the heart of his journey to the Gold Coast. *Black Power* combines the ostensibly objective account of an emerging African nation with the African-American writer's inquiry into the idea of identity rooted in racial origins. Wright's encounters with Africans usually underscore his distance from them, especially when the encounter takes place in the context of a religious tribal/traditional ritual. Wright did not expect his skin color to make Africa more accessible to him. (This would be the assumption of his American readers.) And he was genuinely surprised when certain aspects of Ghanaian culture reminded him of Mississippi. But he was more surprised by the dramatic differences between his own worldview and those of the Western-educated Africans he met. *Black Power* underscores the extent to which race as a component of personal identity is subsumed by a broader, more complex network of collective history and cultural traditions. What set Wright apart from men like Kwame Nkrumah and K. A. Busia was his inability to reconcile their Western education with their adherence to traditional beliefs. These beliefs were antithetical to the modern society he hoped the Ghanaians would build. But too, Wright's resistance to the Africans' religious worldview is related to a personal conviction that such traditions had put millions of black men and women in bondage. Where Wright did find common ground with the Africans of the Gold Coast was in his commitment to a democratic state. In the Gold Coast, Wright saw a parallel to the American experience of a colonial people's struggle to become an independent nation.

In *Lectures in America* and *White Man, Listen!,* discussed in chapter 4, Stein and Wright outline the poetics and politics of modernity and explore the ways in which the two overlap. The Stein lectures account for the originality of her contribution to American literature and claim a place of honor in its history. The Wright lectures revisit the sites of conflict in the modern era: tradition and modernity, the West and the Other. In three lectures, Wright addresses the problem of the developing nations of what we now call the Third World.

In a summary of her aesthetics, Stein returns to the idea of how geography and history influence artists and their art. Unlike the English, whose "daily island life" was essentially confining, the American continent fostered a sense of movement and restlessness. For Stein this demanded new ways of temporal representation. During the composition of *The Making of Americans*, she recalls that the present participle became an obsession. Stein distinguishes her work from that of her predecessors by locating the Aristotelian mandate for a "beginning, middle and end" in opposition to the continuous present: "I could not free myself from the present participle because I felt dimly that I had to know what I knew and I knew that the beginning and middle and ending was not where I began." The basis for the modernist revolution in language was, as Stein tells it, a response to a new world order. Stein's radical experiments with language express an American prerogative: the freedom to accept and reject those aspects of the European past and to express that which was uniquely American. Americans had inherited the English language, but English literary forms could not express the American ethos.

Richard Wright examines racial identity and cultural expression in a lecture on African-American poetry. This lecture, written before his expatriation in 1946, argues that social circumstances rather than racial origins have shaped African-American poetry. Wright argues that the African American's experience, from slave to sharecropper to industrial worker, was the prototypical American, and by extension, modern, experience. After many years abroad he believed that this experience was the sole redeeming feature of American slavery. The lectures Wright delivered to European audiences demonstrate his determination to make visible the ravages of colonialization. *White Man, Listen!* indicts the white world for failing to live up to the principles it professed. These lectures place the experience of the displaced and the discounted at the center of world history. They announce the postcolonial period and outline the issues a truly new world would and still does face.

These late works of nonfiction are more than instances of self-promotion or soapbox oratory. Through these texts Gertrude Stein and Richard Wright engage those conflicts at the center of life in the modern era. Their work "worries" fundamental assumptions about American identity and demonstrates the limits of race, ethnicity, gender, or national origins to define the self. The larger ambition of their work is the exploration of the multifaceted, protean quality of individual identity and its artistic, social, and political expression in the context of a wholly new world.

Innocents Abroad:
Gertrude Stein's *Paris France* and Richard Wright's *Pagan Spain*

And so I am an American and I have lived half my life in Paris, not the half that made me but the half in which I made what I made.

Gertrude Stein

Paris France and *Pagan Spain* extend our understanding of expatriation as a way for American artists to achieve an aesthetic, emotional, and social distance from their native land. These two texts invite us to think about the other side of that distance, Europe in this case, as more than merely a vacuous "euro-world" visible only to the extent that it remains clichéd. To ignore the destination of these narratives is to miss too much. For example, Judith Saunders equated Stein's use of Paris in *Paris France* to Thoreau's use of Walden Pond in *Walden.* Although Stein and Thoreau use these places as mirrors, the qualitative difference between Paris and Walden Pond is crucial; it would be difficult for even the most gifted narcissist to turn Paris into a pond. More important is that Paris places Stein at the center of the modernist movement. Stein's *Paris France,* as opposed to *Walden,* depends on the alternative culture and its values to make its points. The other country provides a rich and densely textured alternative to one's native land so that every aspect of daily life will become an occasion to note the differences.

Key to expatriation for Stein and later for Wright is the way in which the foreign context underscores the idea that social and aesthetic values are constructed. This is not to argue that the French are less racist than Americans, but the fact that many African-Americans noticed how much better they were treated in France was enough to undermine the authority of American racial ideology. Stein notes how aesthetic values are culturally specific. Recalling why so many young Americans found themselves in Paris in the first two decades of this century, she wrote, "Of course they came to France a great many to paint . . . and naturally they could not do that at home, or write they could not do that either. They could be dentists at home . . . Americans were a practical people and dentistry was practical" (19). The implications of cultural relativism for the marginalized such as Gertrude Stein and Richard Wright are crucial. At the beginning of this century, American society barely noted the presence of Jewish, lesbian, or African-American writers, much less what they had to say. In the unfolding American epic they would get scarcely a line. In this context, Gertrude Stein's meditations on Paris in *Paris France* and Richard Wright's account of Spain in the early 1950s, *Pagan Spain,* are illuminating.

In these narratives, Stein and Wright escort us on their journeys and in the process reveal much more about themselves as Americans and writers than about Paris or Madrid. *Paris France* and *Pagan Spain* are intellectual portraits-of-the-artist for these writers who simultaneously distrust and respond to the autobiographical form. But more than solipsistic journeys into the Self, *Paris France* and *Pagan Spain* map the development of the modernist sensibility in its literary and social manifestations.

In lieu of Alice in *The Autobiography of Alice B. Toklas* or the autobiographical Richard in *Black Boy,* the narrators of these texts are closer in time and space to the actual authors precisely because the supposed subject is not the author. Indeed *Paris France* reads like a friendly tête-à-tête on the advantages of French life, while Wright takes us along on interviews, shares his frustrations, and mulls over strange encounters. It is a clever and effective narrative strategy that deflects attention from the authors as autobiographical subjects and focuses instead on their intellectual concerns, which are projected onto the screens of Paris and Spain. Part of their project is to show how writers are born *and* made. In these narratives, Stein and Wright assume we know what they have made; here they attempt to respond to the hows and whys of their making. These accounts provide not simply greater insight into their canonical work; they explore how this work grew out of a need for new and radical forms characteristic of modernism.

On the first page of *Pagan Spain: A Report of a Journey into the Past*, Richard Wright recalls his last meeting with Gertrude Stein. During this visit, just weeks before her death in July 1946, she tells him, "Dick you ought to go to Spain. . . . You'll see the past there, you'll see what the Western world is made of" (1). In August 1954, Wright drove over the French border into the Past. Soon after it was published in 1957, *Pagan Spain* was translated into Spanish; the Spanish critics hated it. Frederico Olivan lost his temper, calling the book "stupid and base . . . a fabric of dull slanders and diatribes against our country" (n. pag.), adding that Spain had freed its slaves before the United States, that Spain had never lynched a black man, and finally that Spain was exporting civilization while Wright's ancestors were naked in African jungles. Wright might have agreed with the spirit if not the specifics of the charge.

Indeed, his journey and the narrative were prompted by an explicit question: How was it that so mighty an empire, one that had initiated the modern world, could in the course of a few centuries become the poor, backward relation of the world it once ruled? For Richard Wright, who covered the Spanish Civil War for the *Daily Worker*, Spain had a special allure. It had financed Columbus's exploration and had conquered much of the so-called New World. But Wright's relationship to that episode in the making of modernity was more complex than Washington Irving's or Ernest Hemingway's. In *Pagan Spain*, Richard Wright, the internationally known writer and the grandson of American slaves, returns to the place where America, and the slave trade on which it was built, began.

The American critics focused on Wright's Marxist slant and on the subjective quality of the text. Black critic Roi Ottley echoed the sentiments of many when he complained that Wright should "stick to fiction" and return to the United States to join the struggle for civil rights. None of Wright's contemporaries noticed the most interesting feature of *Pagan Spain*; in this text Wright reverses the narrative formula of five centuries of European travel writing. *Pagan Spain* is a black American writer's account of European culture. Wright's "exploration" of the "Old World," like that of his European predecessors, betrayed his blindness and prejudices. At the same time, Wright's ethnographer/narrator incorporates a key ingredient of the modernist perspective; in his survey of Spanish life after World War II, Wright exposes the extent to which cultural values—European, like any other—are socially constructed. And unlike many earlier "explorers," Wright did his homework.

Richard Wright's research included three trips to Spain: from August 15 to September 10, 1954; from November 8 to December 17, 1954; and then from February 20 to early April 1955. During these weeks, he visited every major city, monument, and cathedral. He went to bullfights, attended religious festivals, saw gypsies and flamenco dancers. He spoke to a barber in Catalonia, an American matador, wealthy aristocrats, and desperately poor prostitutes. He met Catholics, Protestants, Jews, Republicans and Loyalists, native-born Spaniards and immigrants. For part of the journey, he drove or hired a driver; once or twice he took the train. He stayed in pensions, cheap and average hotels, and once he rented a room with a family. He took photographs and notes, and during the entire journey he traveled more than five thousand miles. The manuscript, completed in March 1957, had 537 pages and included several photographs (Fabre, *Unfinished* 407–13).

Determined to give his account a theoretical frame, Wright incorporated Freudian and Marxist analyses and two critically acclaimed histories of Spain: Americo Castro's *The Structure of Spanish History* and Salvador de Madariaga's *Spain*. Other forms of documentation included a newspaper clipping from the European edition of the *International Herald Tribune*, which supported his own observations of prostitution in Spain, and many personal interviews (189). Between his first and second visit, Wright visited the United Nations Educational, Scientific, and Cultural Organization (UNESCO) library in

Geneva to obtain an economic profile of Spanish life. During his first visit to Spain he was given a text issued by the Spanish government, *Formacion Politica: Lecciones para las Flechas,* parts of which he included in *Pagan Spain.* Indeed critics complained that *Pagan Spain* included more than twenty-five pages of *Formacion Politica.* In a letter to his agent, Paul Reynolds, dated September 19, 1954, Wright stated that he would show "how a non-western people living in Europe work out their life problems" (411). *Pagan Spain* begins with the assumption of cultural difference, which begs the question, different from what?

Wright's perspective is particularly complex because, as he indicated on the dust jacket for the British edition of the text, Spain is where, in George Kent's memorable phrase, "blackness and the adventure of western culture" began. From Robert Park's theory of the Marginal Man, Wright formulates:

> I'm a self-conscious Negro and I'm the product of Western culture, living with white people far from my racial origins. I began to ask myself how did I get there, who brought me there and why? What kind of people were they who dared the oceans to get slaves and sell them? It was in Spain, where tradition has not changed, that I found my answers. . . . But my going to Spain had yet another and deeper meaning, a meaning that I did not know until I got there. I found myself a man freed of traditions, uprooted from my racial heritage, looking at white people who were still caught in their age-old traditions. The white man had unknowingly freed me of my traditional, backward culture, but had clung fiercely to his own. This is the point of *Pagan Spain.* (Fabre, *Richard Wright* 110)

Here Wright sets the stage for the larger, modernist project of *Pagan Spain,* which is to destabilize sacrosanct categories of race, gender, and cultural purity upon which Western civilization is built. The first step in this project is to acknowledge the far-reaching effects of the slave trade, that is, Richard Wright as author of *Pagan Spain.* As he demystifies the revered values of Western culture, Wright reminds us that he is one of the most remarkable consequences of it.

Among the persistent concerns in Wright's late work is how

certain features of American racism, such as economic and political exclusion, can be applied to other groups. Wright's antiessentialist position made him unpopular then as it does now. Without denying the African's specific history of Western violence and oppression, Wright asks that the discussion of blackness be shifted from a biological or spiritual essence to the experience of oppression based on group affiliation; it might include Jews, Spanish Protestants, and Spanish women. In Franco's Spain, Wright identifies what he calls the "white Negro," and very often these are women. Wright arranged to speak to a Protestant woman who had been arrested and detained for teaching the Bible. Before he relates the particulars of this interview he asserts his authority on the subject:

> I am an American Negro with a background of psychological suffering stemming from my previous position as a member of a persecuted racial minority. What drew my attention to the emotional plight of the Protestants in Spain was the undeniable and uncanny psychological affinities that they held in common with American Negroes, Jews and other oppressed minorities. It is another proof, if any is needed today, that the main and decisive aspects of human reactions are conditioned and are not inborn. Indeed, the quickest and simplest way to introduce the subject to the reader would be to tell him that I shall describe some of the facets of psychological problems and emotional sufferings of a group of *white Negroes* whom I met in Spain, the assumption being that Negroes are Negroes because they are *treated* as Negroes. (138)

For many years Wright's informant successfully held Bible classes for impoverished village children. One day, two police officers came during a class and arrested her. Imprisoned for several days she was eventually released but not before learning that the police had an extensive file on her activities. The parallel between the religious intolerance in Spain and the racial intolerance in the United States is underscored in the phrase "the *white Negroes* whom I met in Spain." Despite Wright's antipathy toward the Protestantism in which he was raised, he confessed a "spontaneous and profound sympathy . . . for that exquisite suffering" (138).

Wright returned to the women/black folk parallel in a serendipitous encounter with an American woman. During their chat, she requested that he accompany her to the pension because she intended to check out and was afraid of the landlord. At the pension, there was a loud altercation over the bill. Wright interceded and negotiated the settlement. When it was over, she began to cry. "You are acting like a Negro," Wright scolded. "Raging and wailing and crying won't help you . . . Negroes do that when they are persecuted because of their accident of color. The accident of sex is just as bad. And crying is senseless" (76). You needn't be a black boy from Mississippi to experience a taste of it. You might be a woman, Spanish or American, a Protestant, or a Jew. Intolerance of the "Other" is not bound to "racial" difference. In Spain, that Wright was a man and an American was more important than his skin color.

To further complicate this question, Wright included an encounter that is a critique of his own reading of Spain's intolerance of the Other. Wright arranged to interview a Spanish Jew. Although the young man had recently immigrated to Spain from the Soviet Union, he spoke Spanish fluently. Wright sets the scene: "Jew and Negro, both from backgrounds of persecution, we sat seemingly securely anchored in a twentieth century world of sanity and comfort" (222). But Wright's questions make the man uncomfortable:

"Is there any anti-Semitism in Spain . . . ?"
"No . . . "
"Maybe it was all solved back in 1492 when Ferdinand and Isabel drove the Jews from Spain?"
"Yes . . . You see there are only two thousand five hundred of us here in Spain . . . "
"And since there are practically no Jews in Spain, there can't be a problem, can there?"
"That's right . . . "
"Why did you come to Spain?"
"I like Spain . . . You see my people lived here once . . . My ancestors were here . . . I speak Spanish from them" (223).

Wright was irritated with his informant's unwillingness to discuss Spanish anti-Semitism, so he asked about laws governing marriage between Jews and Catholics, and the role of Jews in Spanish history. The man tried again to explain:

"You see we Jews either had to leave, or turn Catholic, that is become *conversos.* I've come back to the country from which my ancestors were driven centuries ago. *I feel that I am Spanish.*"

"You *want to be* Spanish . . . "

"I'M SPANISH! . . . Names like Perez, Franco, etc., are Jewish names. Toledo is a Jewish word . . . " (224; Wright's emphasis).

And as Wright put it, "a void hung between us" and the meeting ended abruptly (224).

This interview, conducted in late 1954 and early 1955, a mere ten years after the end of World War II, gave Wright an opportunity to note the way the Third Reich had redefined anti-Semitism. That Wright failed to note this is especially interesting because his wife was Jewish. What was the evil of the Inquisition for this young man after Auschwitz? Wright was overly committed to his own view of Spanish racism, and Auschwitz was still too close to be visible. But that the interview remained in the text illustrates the polyvocal feature of *Pagan Spain* that rarely occurred in the typical European travel narrative genre. Mary Pratt observes that Wright, here and elsewhere, exploits heteroglossia in contrast with the more common "monovocal, totalizing forms of discursive authority" (Pratt 162).

In another example linking the plight of black folk and Spanish women, Wright includes a story that was also intended to shock his white readers. One evening he accompanies a white American to see flamenco dancers. Inside the club, Wright notices that his escort is well-known to the young dancers. One asks Wright if he will take her to Africa. Baffled, he asks "S" to explain. "S" furnishes the brothels of North Africa with prostitutes from Spain, and Wright's skin color led the young woman to conclude that he ran a brothel. In transparently affected shock, Wright exclaims: "It hit me like a ton of rock. *White Slavery . . . !*" (184; Wright's emphasis); "This was white slavery, and how simple and open and jolly it was! The women and girls were begging to go; they were hungry" (185). Poverty and ignorance make this situation—unacceptable although not unknown in the United States—not only possible but desirable. And although Wright points to the economic impetus of this practice, he is also interested in the cultural context that makes possible *le monde à l'envers* (white prostitutes/black clientele) and the black folk/Spanish women parallel.

Toward the conclusion of *Pagan Spain*, Wright includes a hymn to Spanish women that registers a genuine sympathy and regard: "Stalwart, they bear the burdens of their poor nation and with but few complaints. They bind up their men's wounds, cater night and day to their childish passions . . . Against impossible odds, they administer the routine of millions of bleak, hungry, and ignorant families . . . the women of Spain make her a nation" (187). And in the context of the entire narrative, Wright finds the Spanish women more willing to discuss the questions he poses. This feature of *Pagan Spain* should, because it is nonfiction, counter the charges of Wright's supposed misogyny.

Just as Wright's *Pagan Spain* points to the relativism of a culture's values, Stein's *Paris France* highlights features of French life that challenge American values. She notes that the French are more solicitous of artists than are Americans. But Stein's most important insights in this regard are in her use of language; indeed, her life's work was to destabilize meaning at its most fundamental level, to illustrate the arbitrary relationship between the sign and the signified. In *Paris France*, Stein employs the anecdote that features a paradox to describe the making of Gertrude Stein, avant-garde writer. Through the anecdote Stein introduces the inherently destabilizing paradox. And through that intrinsically contradictory statement, Stein invites us to reconsider all that is solid.

In *Learning to Curse*, Stephen Greenblatt considers why New Historicism favors the anecdote. For Greenblatt, the anecdote "has at once something of the literary and something that exceeds the literary, a narrative form and a pointed, referential access to what lies beyond or beneath that form" (5). Moreover, according to Joel Fineman, "This conjunction of the literary and the referential . . . functions in the writing of history not as a servant of a grand, integrated narrative of beginning, middle and end but rather as what 'introduces an opening' into that teleological narration" (5). In its insistence on contingency, the anecdote signals a break or disturbance in the "ordinary and well-understood succession of events." Stein's resistance to a "beginning, middle and end" is discussed at length in chapter 4. And her use of the anecdote illustrates quite well the "disturbance" Greenblatt describes. Indeed Stein's anecdotes "introduce an opening" and more; they insist on our inability, and her own, to define or agree upon absolute meaning. Consider the beginning of *Paris France*: "Paris France is exciting and peaceful. I was only four years old when I was first in Paris and talked french there and was photographed there, and ate soup for early breakfast" (1).

The paradoxical observation about Paris is followed by autobiographical detail signaling the relationship not only between Stein and her adopted land but between Stein (as autobiographer and autobiographical subject) *and* paradox. The paradox, the inherent contradiction, is the centerpiece of this narrative. Stein employs this formula throughout *Paris France,* destabilizing wherever possible the very categories that make fixed identity and identification possible. This is nicely illustrated in the anecdote that refers to the subject of her sexuality.

Stein recalls how her servant Hélène had refused to disclose her husband's political party. "What is the matter with you Hélène I said, is it a secret. No Mademoiselle she answered it is not a secret but one does not tell it" (9). Fania Marinoff, visiting from New York, had asked Stein to obtain invitations for her to the other artists in Paris. Stein informed Marinoff that she did not know them: "She could not understand, in New York, she said, if I knew you, I would know them. Yes yes I said but not in Paris . . . because nobody knows anybody whom they do not know" (11). Here Stein imports the distinction between the French verbs, *connaître* and *savoir* that, having no advance warning, results in an apparent tautology. *Connaître* is knowledge that is acquired through familiarity or experience. *Savoir* is knowledge that applies to the realm of the abstract. Both verbs can be correctly translated as "to know," but their applications are so different that they are rarely used interchangeably. As she does everywhere, Stein puts the code in a code.

Stein's insistence on privacy had its source in her desire to conceal, to some extent, the nature of her relationship with Alice Toklas. *Women of the Left Bank: Paris, 1900–1940* by Sheri Benstock is a detailed discussion of the lesbian community of that period. There is a striking contrast between the discretion of the Stein/Toklas relationship and the rather flamboyant behavior of women like Natalie Barney. Critics such as Anna Gibbs and Elizabeth Fifer have shed valuable light on the erotic dimensions of Stein's work. But on the subject of her sexuality, Stein adopted the French attitude; it was not a secret, but one did not tell it. This anecdote comments on the open secret of her relationship to Alice and at the same time notes how this relationship would have been difficult in the United States where everybody knew everybody, even when they did not know them.

Through another anecdote featuring paradox, Stein describes a French attitude she finds both baffling and intriguing. When her dog Basket died, a French friend urged her to get another dog who resembled Basket, to then name it Basket and soon and she would not know which Basket it was. But Picasso objected: "Why supposing I were to die, you would go out on the street and sooner or later you would meet a Pablo but it would not be I and it would not be the same" (70). She compromised and "tried to have the same and not to have the same" (70). They named the new dog Basket, "I cannot say that the confusion between the old and the new has yet taken place but certainly le roi est mort vive le roi, is a normal attitude of mind" (70).

This anecdote adds another dimension to the old problem, the arbitrary nature between the name and that to which it refers. For "le roi est mort vive le roi" introduces another aspect of identity, that of the role. Not all Pablos are Picassos, and the deceased Basket is not the new Basket; but the new Basket's role is that of his predecessor. If this "confusion" is effective, is there a serious difference between the old and the new? And how much does one's role have to do with one's identity? This anecdote echoes Michael North's observation that in "Melanctha" Stein, "invites her predominantly white readership to

North
A

identify with the characters and thus play a black role, and yet presenting race as a role seems an open invitation to consider it as culturally constituted and perhaps to consider gender a role as well" (70).
Stein's anecdotes open up the questions; they do not answer them.

It is not surprising to find Stein and Wright, as Americans, at-
tracted to the creole aspects in French and Spanish culture. Paul
Gilroy has noted that the cultural and political exchanges and transformations he finds especially appropriate for the culture of what he
terms the black Atlantic are inadequately theorized by terms like
"creolization" and "syncretism" (*Black Atlantic* 74–75). I quite
agree. My use of the term "creole" in this discussion follows Albert
Murray's in *The Omni Americans* and will, I hope, be clear from the
context. Gertrude Stein had an in-depth knowledge of this feature of
French life, and she relates it through a series of anecdotes, on food
and dogs and colloquialisms, topics considered trivial for most critics. Using the anecdote to "introduce an opening" Stein invites us to
think about how these stories relate to the development of her avant-
garde writing. She notes how adept the French are at incorporating
foreign cultural elements so completely that their origins are all but
forgotten. We learn that the croissant was brought to France by
Marie Antoinette, "they took it over so completely so completely that
it became French so completely French that no other nation questions it" (46). Just as the French have adapted the word "pastime" to
"*passetemps*," so too have they taken foreign breeds of dogs and
made them over in their own special way. So much so that she was
surprised to learn that the poodle is not an indigenous French breed
(33–36).

Just as she played with the definitions of "savoir" and "connaître"
to make a point about kinds of knowledge, Stein found these instances of creolization a practice important to the development of
her own style. Once in a restaurant she had overheard the phrase
avant que l'amitié ne flétrît, les fleurs de l'amitié flétrirent, "before
friendship faded, the flowers of friendship faded" (Faÿ 146). She
later used it, changing the syntax and ultimately its meaning: "before the flowers of friendship faded friendship faded"; this phrase is
as explicitly Gertrude Stein as her autograph. In *Everybody's Autobi-*

ography, Stein referred to a Frenchman who was unemployed as an "out of work." This is the literal translation of the French noun *chômeur.* Stein simply turned the adjectival phrase into a noun. In *Lucy Church Amiably* (1927), the male characters are named John Mary and Simon Therese because "It always pleases me that French boys are often called Jean-Marie, you can use a female name to go with a man's name, it hallows the male name to add the female name to it" (68–69). In English this coupling is strange and disconcerting, which was part of Stein's project; verbal configurations that defamiliarize the familiar are a regular feature of modernist writing. But this example also comments on a culture's values: why is a conventional practice in France a serious aberration in the United States?

Richard Wright was fascinated by the creole quality of Spanish culture. Indeed, among the reasons he chose to write a book on Spain are the heterogeneous origins of Spanish culture. One of Wright's most important sources, Americo Castro's *The Structure of Spanish History,* explores the multicultural quality of Spain. Castro was interested in the Jewish and Muslim influences on the formation of Spanish character. The "pagan" in Wright's title refers to the not purely Christian elements of Spanish culture. When Wright sent his agent, Paul Reynolds, the manuscript, he included an engraving of Santiago de Compostella overcoming a Moor (Fabre, *Unfinished* 608, n.5). This image illustrated the essence of Castro's argument; the Spanish character was developed through an extended and violent encounter of the Christian with the "Other." And that the "Other" was dark-skinned was particularly important to Richard Wright. The only footnote in *Pagan Spain* refers to the "pagan" underpinnings of Spanish culture. At lunch with a Spanish family, Wright mentioned that the origin of the word "olé" was Moorish, meaning "for God's sake." Wright uses a direct quote from Castro: "And I believe that in many instances behind the Christian God vibrates the echo of Allah, present in the interjection ole! (*wa-l-lah,* "for God's sake") with which audiences shout their encouragement to dancers and bull-fighters" (Castro 113). Wright's incredulous hosts stare open-mouthed, "They had been uttering the pagan religious phrases of the Moors and never known it!" (90). (In this example of creolization,

Wright saw a parallel to American English. Consider the frequency with which Yiddish or "black English" is incorporated into "mainstream" American speech.) For Wright this was especially striking because the word had survived long after the Moor had been defeated and expelled from Spain. By calling attention to the creole features of French and Spanish cultures, Stein and Wright further destabilize the notion of racial, ethnic, linguistic, and cultural purity. More important, this move also undermines the idea of Europe as the unique source of American origins and identity.

The composition of both *Pagan Spain* and *Paris France* was prompted by war. The relationship between modern warfare and modernist poetics and politics is beyond the scope of this study. The important point here is simply that these wars, World War I, the Spanish Civil War, and World War II, contributed to the shifts in perspectives Stein and Wright had begun to, or would afterwards, explore. These shifts in worldview, beginning with World War I, marked a turning point in Western and global history. Walter Benjamin's assessment is perfect: "A generation that had gone to school on a horse-drawn streetcar now stood under the open sky in a countryside in which nothing remained unchanged but the clouds, and beneath these clouds, in a field of force of destructive torrents and explosions, was the tiny, fragile human body" (84).

Not quite two decades would pass before Spain became the site of this transformation. During the first half of World War I, Stein and Toklas had taken refuge on the island of Majorca off the Costa Brava (neighboring Ibiza, where fourteen years later, Walter Benjamin spent the first years of his exile). In 1937, Richard Wright attended the second American Writers Conference, which was comprised of liberals and Communist Party members. One event featured a film, *The Spanish Earth*. Scenes from this film, shot on the front lines of the Spanish Civil War, were followed by discussions of the writer's responsibility to combat fascism. Lillian Hellman, Ernest Hemingway, and Archibald MacLeish participated. To complete the circle of coincidence, Max White, a delegate from California, met Wright and was so impressed by his intelligence and his admiration for Stein that he wrote and told her about him (Fabre, *Unfinished* 141, 549 n.4). For Richard

Wright, these many threads came together eighteen years later as he prepared to write *Pagan Spain*. *Paris France* was published in 1940, just as the French made the devil's deal with the Third Reich in what was called the "drôle de paix."

Benjamin's assessment of how World War I left its participants mute is an important piece to the picture of modernist poetics and politics, for the presence of war in these texts points to an instability whose implications are felt on every level of human activity. In the decade before his death, Wright explored the transformation that made former colonies into sovereign states. In the last years of her life, Stein's work took on a radical political dimension. *Pagan Spain* and *Paris France* explore the disruptive quality of war, lament its capacity to destroy, and celebrate the possibility of beginning anew.

In 1937, Wright, then a reporter for the Harlem Bureau of the *Daily Worker*, had published a series of articles on the Spanish Civil War. These pieces praise the efforts of the Black American soldiers of the Abraham Lincoln Brigade who fought alongside the Loyalists. In one article, Wright interviewed a young black soldier from Brooklyn whose career in the Loyalist army symbolized the achievement still elusive for blacks in the Jim Crow American armed forces; in less than a year, Walter Garland had risen to the rank of lieutenant in charge of an American training base in Spain. Wright's enthusiasm for the Loyalists and pride in the African Americans who fought for their cause is everywhere apparent in these articles. Wright saw the implications of a war against fascism for African Americans; this issue would be exacerbated during and following World War II. Through the lens of a foreign civil war, Wright saw a struggle for oppressed people everywhere. Two decades later, *Pagan Spain* began with this confession: "The fate of Spain had hurt me, had haunted me; I had never been able to stifle a hunger to understand what had happened there and why" (2).

Wright's decision to write a book on Spain illustrates how the volatility of the postwar period animated him. By 1954 he had lived in France for eight years and had completed—in addition to a great number of articles, book reviews, and essays—two novels, *The Outsider* (1953) and *Savage Holiday* (1954), and a work of nonfiction,

Black Power (1954), none of which were received with the enthusiasm of *Native Son* or *Black Boy*. Although Wright was willing to forgo commercial success, Paul Reynolds Jr. suggested that he work on a novel set during the Civil War or on the African-American community in Paris. But in reply Wright admitted: "I'm inclined to feel that I ought not to work right now on a novel. This does not mean that I'm giving up writing fiction, but, really, there are so many more exciting and interesting things happening now in the world that I feel sort of dodging them if I don't say something about them" (Fabre, *Unfinished* 407). Wright's desire to explore the "exciting and interesting things happening now in the world" was linked to the spirit of revolution he pursued in *Black Power* and *The Color Curtain*. Richard Wright refused to be the "Negro" writer, and he realized long before it became obvious to others the ways in which the cultural media of African Americans could and would contribute to the global transformation we now refer to as the postcolonial period. For example, the Civil Rights movement in the United States had direct implications for independence movements in Africa and Asia. But Wright paid dearly for this decision; critics, both black and white, complained and castigated the expatriate for being out of touch with the source of his creativity. Wright's struggle with an inherently racist audience and publishing establishment was symptomatic of the prewar mentality, the perspective he wanted his work to change. His writing on the transformation of Africa was a contribution (one of many) to the new world order. In encounters like the following, he would experience both his privilege as an American and what he felt to be his responsibility as a writer.

   This strangely moving episode came about when Wright telephoned a woman he had met on a train. During that journey, she had observed him taking notes and asked about his work. They spent much of the long ride engaged in conversation and, although the language proved a barrier, the woman's generosity (she gave him a book of flamenco lyrics) and candor had impressed him. When he telephoned, she invited him to dinner. Wright learned that Lita's husband had been killed by Franco's forces during the Civil War. Wright asked, "How is life here?" to which Lita replied, "Bad . . . Hard, very hard. We eat, that's all. We eat a little" (170). The tiny living room became profoundly quiet. A guest sang a flamenco verse that provoked Lita's rage:

"Franco!" she croaked with fury. *"Comprende?"*
"Si, Señora," I said.
"Hombre malo," she said.
She lifted her arms and her thin white hands made a fluttering movement and her mouth imitated the roar of plane engines . . .
"BOOOOOM! BOOOOOOM!"
"La guerre," I said.
"Si Señor," she said. *"Libertad terminada . . . La mitad de la gente española no come,"* she hissed. (172)

The somber atmosphere was eventually dispelled by songs and pantomimes; at one point Wright got down on all fours and imitated a charging bull. And when he announced that he had to take an early morning train (he had spent the entire evening and wee hours of the morning there), the party accompanied him to the station: "I shook hands all around, then climbed aboard. I opened a window and looked down into their naked pleading eyes and I knew that this love that they were demonstrating was not for me alone; it was an appeal to that world that they had never seen and whose reality they had almost begun to doubt. I represented that world to them. I took out my fountain pen and waved gently to them. 'Para *usted,*' I whispered to them" (175). No passage better illustrates what Wright felt his role to be. He was a symbol of a freer more humane world. The final gesture, the fountain pen, the whispered phrase, was the fitting response.

As *Paris France* was published in 1940, Stein's American critics expected some direct response to the European crisis. Stein went on record saying there would not be another European war, and the first part of the narrative is blissfully oblivious to those events that had kept her from resuming her life in Paris. In the early months of the war, Stein and Toklas received a military pass to visit Paris for thirty-six hours. They took two paintings and some documents. They did not see Paris again for five years (Mellow 434–47). But the second half of the text is dominated by the presence of the war. Stein would later devote an entire book to the five years she and Alice Toklas spent in the country trying to remain invisible. What culminates in *Wars I Have Seen* (1945) begins in the final pages of *Paris France*. In the presence of the war, Stein's equanimity begins to waver; even as she tries to assume the sangfroid of her neighbors, her fears and apprehension find expression through an interpolated tale.

The "Helen Button" episode is listed as a separate item in the *Yale Catalogue*, suggesting that it was not composed as part of the text of *Paris France* (Bridgman 298). Still, it is especially effective in this context. Stein introduces the story by pondering what a child feels during wartime. The episode describes a few experiences of a young French girl living in the country during "wartime." Helen Button, the autobiographical character, and her dog William take frequent walks, and during these excursions the events of the story take place. They encounter a bottle standing straight up in the middle of the road filled with some kind of fluid the color of which might be green, blue, or black. "They did not look back at the bottle. But of course it was still there because they had not touched it. That is wartime" (82). The order of daily life is strangely out of place. Helen's observations focus on aspects of village life that the war has disrupted. Boys riding bicycles that are too big for them attest to the fact that their older brothers and fathers have been sent off to war. The war has a pernicious effect on everyone's imagination. Helen's friend Emil has a dog "who had been born in the country against which they were fighting" (83). Emil does not know if he can love his dog even though she is loyal and affectionate, and Helen imagines its kafkaesque metamorphosis: "It was not true of course, it was not true but Helen said to herself, I was watching the dog . . . changing . . . and it was a man . . . an enemy man" (86).

Similarly Helen sees an old horse pulling a wagon on which lay a huge dead animal: "it was enormous and it was dead" (89). "It did not have a tail and it did not have any ears. It was an enormous animal and it was war-time. Helen did not really see it but she told herself about it" (90). This is a metaphor for war and its effects on the imagination: without the capacity to hear or for balance, the animal represents the extent to which fear incapacitates human activity. That the creature is dead is the only hopeful note in the story. Only a return to an ordered life breaks the spell: "So now it was still war-time and Helen began to go to school too. So for her war-time was over" (92).

"War-time" is characterized by uncertainty and rupture, features characteristic of the modernist aesthetic. Through this interpolated tale, Stein was able to express the apprehension brought on by the threat of war without altering the overall portrait. This illustrated another quality she found admirable about the French: "The French do love to say a thing and say it completely. That is the reason that once a thing is completely named it does no longer worry them" (96). This glib response ultimately proved inadequate; Stein's "war-time" fears and anxiety are expressed in *Mrs. Reynolds* and in *Wars I Have Seen*.

In *Paris France*, Stein relies on the paradox and the apparent conflict of opposites, a strategy that animated Stein's creativity. *Paris France* establishes the relationship between her American identity as expressed in *The Geographical History of America* and her need to live in France: "everybody who writes is interested in living inside themselves in order to tell what is inside themselves. That is why writers have to have two countries, the one where they belong and the one in which they live really. The second one is romantic, it is separate from themselves, it is not real but it is really there" (2). Distance is preserved by living in a place where one's native language is not spoken and where evidence of one's own history is missing. France also provided freedom from an external reality that threatened to subsume the artist's identity. "When you are you in your own civilisation you are apt to mix yourself up too much with your own civilisation" (Stein, *What Are Masterpieces* 63). Richard Wright noted this freedom from one's own civilization while he was reading Stein's *Narration*. Simply put, "One of the things I have liked all these years is to be surrounded by people who knew no english. It has left me more intensely alone with my eyes and my english" (Stein, *Autobiography* 70).

The French recognized the preeminent place of the artist in society in a way that stood in sharp contrast to the American attitude.

Stein observes: "it is quite true even in a garage an academician and a woman of letters take precedence even of millionaires or politicians . . . after all the way everything is remembered is by the writers and painters of the period, . . . and in realizing that the french show their usual sense of reality" (21). Many years later, James Baldwin made the same observation in his essay, "The Discovery of What It Means to Be an American," On being an American writer in Europe, Baldwin agreed with Stein's earlier observations, "The American writer, in Europe, is released, first of all, from the necessity of apologizing for himself. . . . It is not necessary for him, there, to pretend to be something that he is not, for the artist does not encounter in Europe the same suspicion he encounters here" (6). Paris provided the modern artist with the "background of tradition of profound conviction that men, women and children do not change" and that "tradition, and their private life and the soil which always produces something, that is what counts" (10–11).

But why did Gertrude Stein, so firmly identified with America, the twentieth century, and radically new literature, need such a tradition-bound atmosphere? Again Stein saw in the apparent contradiction the dialectical reply. Paris was a place where tradition was so firm that "they [the French] could look modern without being different, and where their acceptance of reality was so great that they could let anyone have the emotion of unreality" (18). There was also the French attitude toward foreigners: "After all to the french the difference between being a foreigner and being an inhabitant is not very serious" (18). This last observation was changing even as she wrote those lines; the antiforeign, anti-Semitic policies she had escaped were evidence of the end of an era in France and in Europe. In one of the most poignant passages from *The Making of Americans,* she describes how it felt to be Gertrude Stein in America:

It takes time to make queer people. . . . Custom, passion, and a feel for mother earth are needed to breed vital singularity in any man, and alas, how poor we are in all these three. Brother Singulars, we are misplaced in a generation that knows not Joseph. We flee before the disapproval of our cousins, the courageous condescension of our friends who gallantly sometimes agree to walk the streets with us, from all them who never any way can understand why such ways and not the others are so dear to us, we fly to the kindly comfort of an older world accustomed to take all manner of strange forms into its bosom. (21)

Put another way, "It was not what France gave you but what it did not take away from you that was important" (Stein, *What Are Masterpieces* 70).

The origins for *Paris France* are found in a small essay composed in 1936–37, "An American and France." This is the beginning:

America is my country and Paris is my home town and it is as it has come to be. After all anybody is as their land and air is. Anybody is as the sky is low or high, the air heavy or clear and anybody is as there is wind or no wind there. It is that which makes them and the arts they make and the work they do and the way they eat and the way they drink and the way they learn and everything. And so I am an American and I have lived half my life in Paris, not the half that made me but the half in which I made what I made. (Stein, *What Are Masterpieces* 62)

Stein's position is deliberately difficult to locate. She asserts her possession of both places: "America is my country and Paris is my home town." The conjunction "and," as opposed to "but," indicates that they are equally important. She insists upon the influence of geography on the individual, but her statement lacks specificity: Is the "anybody" Stein? Is the "land" and "air" American or Parisian? To which place do the "land" and "air" refer? Again affirming her American identity, she adds that she has lived half her life in Paris. The "land" and "air" of the previous paragraph can apply to America and Paris: "It is that which makes them and the arts they make and the work they do." America inspired the literature she would write, but writing was not something Americans did at home; at home they were dentists or, as in Stein's case, physicians. She concludes: "Not the half that made me but the half in which I made what I made." Stein's portrait of France is not just a portrait of the artist; it incorporates a far more complex modernist view of identity that at its most basic is dependent on a dialectic. *Paris France,* as would *Pagan Spain* fourteen years later, revealed the extent to which the locus of modernism (if it can be located) was in the dynamic relationship between the self and the "Other."

Among the many writerly projects Wright incorporated into *Pagan Spain* is the revision of earlier Spanish narratives by two of his compatriots. *Pagan Spain* begins with a description of Wright's last conversation with Gertrude Stein. Through Stein, we are reminded of one of her most gifted pupils who, like Richard Wright, was fascinated by Spain. Wright probably met Ernest Hemingway in 1937, at the second American Writers' Conference (Fabre, *Unfinished* 141). Hemingway had come to describe the Spanish Civil War and to plead the Loyalists' cause. Michel Fabre has unearthed this description of that event from Wright's unpublished papers: "Ernest Hemingway, looking in person like a retired Illinois business man, brought vivid word pictures of battles between the loyalists and fascists in Spain. . . . It was the first time the sensitive and legendary Hemingway had ever faced an audience from a platform, and his determination to tell the truth about fascism was apparent in his impassioned sincerity" (Fabre, *Wright Books* 71). These details suggest that the origins of *Pagan Spain* were as literary as they were political. In all of Wright's work, the two were inextricably bound, but during his voyages to Spain, Wright was especially conscious of this literary tradition and of his place in it.

Wright begins, however, with that first American writer of Spanish narratives, Washington Irving. In Granada, Wright, with *The Alhambra* tucked under his arm, visited the Alhambra and the Generalife palace. The distance between the perspective of the two writers is vividly illustrated in their descriptions of the palace. This is Irving's:

High above the Alhambra, on the breast of the mountain, amidst embowered gardens and stately terraces, rise the lofty towers and white walls of the Generalife; a fairy palace, full of storied recollections . . . Here were preserved the portraits of many who figured in the romantic drama of the Conquest . . . Ferdinand and Isabella, Ponce de Leon, the gallant marquis of Cadiz, and Garcilaso de la Vega, who slew the Tarfe and Moor, a champion of Herculean Strength. (Irving 200)

And this is Wright's:

I wandered over the ruins of Alhambra and Generalife, . . . and walked through the palace, the fortress and the summer gardens, then among the vast brick battlements erected centuries earlier by the Moors. . . . These relics represented the terminal point of influence of the East and Africa in Europe. Since the vanquishing of the Moors by Ferdinand and Isabella . . . the tide of history had reversed itself and Europe, with a long and bloody explosion, had hurled itself upon the masses of mankind in Asia and Africa and the then unknown Americas. (162)

Unlike Irving, who "had been charmed by this monstrous pile of dead glory and had woven romantic tales about it" (162), Wright will not accept this interpretation of history. Instead Irving's "romantic drama of the Conquest" becomes Wright's "long and bloody explosion." In revising this passage of *The Alhambra*, Wright places his own work in the context of a tradition in which he obviously shares, and he illustrates how his vision, born of his own particularly American experience, contributes to that tradition. Here Wright is two decades ahead of those historians who after the American Civil Rights movement would see the history of Western civilization in a completely new light.

Wright names Hemingway in *Pagan Spain*, but he did not have to; simply to describe a bullfight would have been enough to invoke his memory. Richard Wright's account of the bullfight is both indebted to and a tribute to Hemingway. But when we compare the two descriptions, an important difference emerges. One of Hemingway's best descriptions of the bullfight is from *The Sun Also Rises*. Hemingway's focus is on the matador and how the act of encountering the bull reveals the passion and courage of the man. Similarly, Richard Wright is impressed by the bravery of the young matador he witnessed in the ring; but this is not his focal point. Consider the following passages, the first of which is from *The Sun Also Rises*: "Out in the center of the ring Romero profiled in front of the bull, drew the sword out from the folds of the muleta, rose on his toes, and sighted along the blade. The bull charged as Romero charged" (218). This is Wright's description of this same moment: "Chamaco's left hand now grasped the muleta firmly; he turned away from the bull, looking at him sideways, letting the red cloth drop below his left knee. He now lifted his gleaming sword chin high and sighted along the length of it, pointing its sharp, steel tip at the tormented and bloody mound of wounds on the bull's back. Chamaco's left hand twitched the cloth, citing the bull. The bull saw it and charged. Chamaco charged, meeting the bull" (111–12). Just as Wright had amended Irving's version of the Generalife, here too, his inclusion of "the tormented and bloody mound of wounds on the bull's back" is the difference between his own account of the bullfight and that of his literary predecessor and compatriot.

As an emendation to Hemingway's description, Wright focuses on the sociological and pathological dimensions of the ritual for its participants. Going further than Hemingway, for whom the bullfight expresses individual heroism, Wright sees it as a "man made agony to assuage the emotional needs of men" (112). Wright agreed that the matador represented a masculine heroic, but he sought to understand how this ritual functioned in the context of an oppressive society. That Wright could impart this meaning to the bullfight is not surprising to anyone familiar with his work. But by addressing this subject, so incontestably Hemingway's, Wright moves the focal point from the poetics of modernism to its political implications, further emphasizing the African American's experience and contribution to American history and his own contribution to American literature.

American Odyssey:
Richard Wright's *Black Power* and Gertrude Stein's *Everybody's Autobiography*

To feel oneself in two places at once, at home and abroad, is almost to feel as two persons and thus to acquire a skepticism about the possibility of ever having an identity, if that means being just one thing.

Michael North

This observation articulates one of the most important features of the modernist sensibility for Gertrude Stein and Richard Wright in both poetics and politics. Stein and Wright were, given the facts of American life, in a better position than most to experience "the variability and indeterminacy of human identity" (North 67). Even though there is abundant evidence for this in their canonical works, the homecoming narratives offer remarkable insight into the creative encounter with the indeterminacy of human identity. Stein's *Everybody's Autobiography* chronicles a seven-month journey back to the United States after a thirty-year absence. *Black Power* is Wright's account of life in the Gold Coast on the eve of that colony's independence from Britain. I read both texts as "journeys home" where the meaning of "home" and "self" are difficult to define. Stein's *Everybody's Autobiography* and Wright's *Black Power* pose a number of questions: How much of who we are is determined by our "ancestors" and our "native land?" Is it possible to leave one's homeland and remain of that place if not in it? Or, in Wright's case, is it possible to feel "one's roots" as one African put it, after a four-century hiatus? It should come as no surprise that these questions are posed by the authors of *The Making of Americans* and *Native Son*. Americans have always been uneasy on the issue of origins; how much more so for those whose race or ethnicity make this problem more complicated. Identity animated their curiosity and creativity because the questions of origins and the authority they confer are at the complex center of modernity.

To begin, there are important differences between these two texts. Stein's *Everybody's Autobiography* recounts a journey to her native land, and *Black Power* is an account of Wright's first visit to the African continent. In the Gold Coast, he was an outsider in ways that Stein, even after a three-decade absence, was not in the United States. Still, the comparison works for a number of reasons. For both authors the relationship to the destination is complicated by a priori assumptions that are central to the question of identity. Stein had lived in France for thirty years, how American could she be? And in the context of American racist ideology, Wright's African ancestry would *naturally* make his visit to the Gold Coast a kind of homecoming. (Comedian Richard Pryor makes this point in a skit where he and a white American are visitors at a hotel in Africa. When the two are approached by a group of Africans speaking a native language, the white American asks Pryor to translate). Each writer handles these simplistic and crushingly potent assumptions with remarkable honesty and intelligence. In the following discussion, we accompany these intrepid travelers as they explore, with long outdated maps, the idea of identity, of authenticating origins, and of home.

One of the most astonishing events in Gertrude Stein's long and eventful life was the phenomenal popularity of *The Autobiography of Alice B. Toklas*. *The Autobiography* ran into four printings by 1935, and its first printing of 5,400 copies was sold out by August 22, 1933, nine days before the book was officially published (Mellow 351–78). The text took six weeks to compose and bore little resemblance to the experimental writing to which she had devoted her life. Indeed the popularity of *The Autobiography* provoked a rather serious identity crisis in its author. And one of the consequences of both *The Autobiography*'s success and Stein's crisis was her seven-month lecture tour throughout the United States. Out of this experience came three more texts: *Everybody's Autobiography, Lectures in America,* and *The Geographical History of America, Or the Relation of the Human Nature to the Human Mind.* Through these narratives, Stein attempts to come to terms with the paradox of her relationship to America and its implications for her work and her sense of self.

In October 1934, after thirty years, Gertrude Stein came home. During her journey throughout the United States, she gave numerous public lectures, viewed a production of her play *Four Saints in Three Acts,* and conducted a seminar at the University of Chicago. She met film stars Charlie Chaplin and Mary Pickford and writers Anita Loos, Marianne Moore, and Dashiell Hammett. She had tea with Eleanor Roosevelt, attended a Yale/Dartmouth football game, and toured Chicago's black ghetto in a squad car. And she returned to the places of her past. She spent the Christmas holidays with family members in Pikesville, Maryland, and visited the Swett School in East Oakland. Although Stein reveled in celebrity, the journey also exacerbated the personal crisis provoked by the commercial success of *The Autobiography of Alice B. Toklas.* Written in the afterglow of her triumphant homecoming, *Everybody's Autobiography* engages the contradictions of Stein's life: she was an American who had spent half of her life abroad, and she had achieved recognition and financial success from the publication of a text that did not represent her contribution to twentieth-century literature. The narrative oscillates between a cheerful travelogue and a more somber meditation on the meaning of identity and perhaps ultimately its inaccessibility to anyone.

The complexity of *Everybody's Autobiography* is rooted in Stein's simultaneous resistance and capitulation to the exigencies of time and place to define herself. A desire to account for the facts of her life competes with an unyielding struggle against the definitive. The problem of identity (all its components, national, gender, ethnic) and artistic integrity are at the center of every contradiction. But just as she would later use aspects of life in France to justify her creative activity, Stein found a quintessential instability at the heart of American life that she claimed as the source of her artistic originality. And this indeterminacy is the locus of her meditations on all aspects of identity.

As if in a final reply to those who would impugn her claim to an American passport, Stein wrote *The Geographical History of America, Or the Relation of Human Nature to the Human Mind.* In it she argues that the creative aspect of consciousness, the "human mind," exists independently of the more mundane aspect she terms "human nature." Creativity takes place in the context of "immediate existing," whereas "human nature" is related to identity and is determined and defined by memory and external recognition. Although her theory insists on this division in consciousness, it is clear that in Stein's own mind, the two are never separate or unequal: "The human mind has nothing to do with age. As I say so tears come into my eyes" (63). The larger ambition of this text is to link timelessness and indeterminacy with America, the America that made Gertrude Stein and ultimately with the Gertrude Stein who made American modernism. Stein's relationship to her American identity had to be free of a residency requirement, and after 1904, it was. It had to be an unfinished, unorthodox work in progress, which in fact it was. *The Geographical History of America* illustrates her actual and aesthetic relationship to her native land.

Formally, *The Geographical History of America* illuminates Stein's thinking in *Everybody's Autobiography.* *The Geographical History* violates the notion of sequential time. There are a dozen chapters entitled "Chapter I." A "Chapter V" is followed by a "Chapter III." A "Part IV" is followed by another "Part IV." "Chapter II" follows "Chapter VI," which in its entirety reads, "I could have begun with Chapter I but anybody even I have had enough of that" (95). (Note the visual pun between "I" referring to the number one and "I" referring to herself.) Similarly she writes, "There is no reason why chapters should succeed each other since nothing succeeds another, not now any more" (90). The "human mind" must resist constraints imposed by time, memory, and identity to write, in this case, autobiography. Traditional autobiography, she claims, has "nothing to do with the human mind" (89). Formally, Stein undermined the use of time as an organizational device, but she could never completely divorce its antitemporal form from its content that is rooted in history. Toward the conclusion, there are a number of sections entitled, "Autobiography I" and "Autobiography number II." These sections continue her ruminations on the human mind, but her reflections include memories. She recalls the problem of representing time in *The Making of Americans,* "I remember so well always saying in the Making of Americans then knowing not knowing but having then the difficulty of being sure that then was then" (185). In "Autobiography number V," she recalls studying philosophy at college, and in the next section, "Autobiography one again," she, without naming him, recalls Picasso's divorce (186–87).

Even in outline, Stein was unable to write autobiography that did not depend on memory. But in the effort to do so, she made clear the limits of that endeavor. By calling into question the notion of identity, memory, and time as fixed, she reminds her audience that autobiography is never a faithful rendering of life. Toward the end of *The Geographical History* Stein writes, "Ordinarily anybody finishes anything. But not in writing. In writing not any one finishes anything. That is what makes a master-piece what it is that there is no finishing" (230). And the text aptly concludes, "I am not sure that this is the not the end" (243).

Stein's insistence on the literariness of autobiography, coupled with the paucity of autobiographical detail, have made *Everybody's Autobiography* a book few critics have taken seriously. Those who do focus on the aesthetic theory it is supposed to illustrate. For example, Shirley Neuman demonstrates the ways in which *Everybody's Autobiography* illustrates Stein's aesthetic theories that were in turn a result of her scientific training. But every formal innovation in *Everybody's Autobiography* is grounded in its rich and varied content. The "unappreciated depths" in this narrative can only be glimpsed through the contradictions that emerge from the tension between form and content. A particularly nice example of this is the autobiography's title. The oxymoron reminds us that this work, like *The Autobiography,* is a literary construct, not a factual report. The

term "everybody" recalls the universal, democratic impulse characteristic of American thought and literary expression, while the term
"autobiography" preserves the individuality so dear to the American
"everybody." And with Walt Whitman in mind, Stein's title refers to
the American sojourn during which she spoke to "everybody" and
felt herself well qualified to write their autobiography.

The title is also an important sign for the direction of Stein's
meditations on identity. The proper noun is replaced with the all-
inclusive pronoun "everybody." If, Stein argues, an autobiography
can be written without a proper noun, what then does that suggest
about the notion of a proper noun with its specific demands of time
and place? In the third paragraph of *Everybody's Autobiography*, she
raises the question again with a slightly different emphasis. Recalling Alice's response to the title of her "autobiography," Stein wrote:
"In the first place she did not want it to be Alice B. Toklas, if it has
to be at all it should be Alice Toklas and in the French translation it
was Alice Toklas . . . but in America and in England too Alice B.
Toklas was more than Alice Toklas. Alice Toklas never thought so
and always said so" (3). Neither Alice nor her life, as narrated in *The
Autobiography*, would have been diminished by omitting her middle
initial. (Notice the pun on "B" and "be.") Insisting on the name that
refers to the person or the initial that refers to the name does not
make for a truer portrait. These examples illustrate Stein's methodology in *Everybody's Autobiography*; even as she locates the source of
her creativity in her American identity, both noun and adjective
must remain unfixed, unstable, in flux, very much like the aesthetic
she helped to create.

Responding to the charge that after thirty years of expatriation,
she had lost her roots, Stein wrote:

I think I must have had a feeling that it had happened or I should not
have come back. . . . I went to California. I saw it and felt it and it had a
tenderness and a horror too. Roots are so small and dry when you have
them and they are exposed to you. You have seen them on a plant and
sometimes they seem to deny the plant if it is vigorous. . . . Well, we're not
like that if you think about it, we take our roots with us. I always knew that

a little and now I know it wholly. I know because you can go back to where they are and they can be less real to you than they were three thousand, six thousand miles away. Don't worry about your roots. . . . The essential thing is to have the feeling that they exist, that they are somewhere. They will take care of themselves, and they will take care of you, too, though you may never know how it has happened. To think of going back for them is to confess that the plant is dying. (Brinnin 339)

This expresses very clearly Stein's relationship to America; it thrives in her heart and mind, and more vigorously than it might were she compelled to live there.

The discussion of roots is multivalent in the context of African-American history and identity. Gertrude Stein's family immigrated to the United States in the nineteenth century. But Richard Wright's African ancestors may have landed at Jamestown in 1619; and if one's claim to American identity is linked to the number of generations, Wright's is clearly the strongest. Slavery and racist terrorism worked effectively to alienate African Americans from the culture and nation they too built. It is no wonder that many African Americans celebrate their African ancestry, because, as Charles Johnson's runaway slave narrator Andrew Hawkins/William Harris puts it, "There is no history worth mentioning, only family scenarios of deprivation and a bitter struggle-and failure-against slavery" (Johnson 132). Of course there is a history worth mentioning; indeed, in *Black Power*, Richard Wright will argue that American history is the history of African Americans. *Black Power* begins with these questions: What if one's roots are in Mississippi but every intricate fiber in the social fabric conspires to conceal this bond? What if one's rootedness in America goes back four centuries but a racist society accepts Africa as the only legitimate homeland for black Americans? How can the African American honor his/her African origins when that identity is rooted in a profoundly racist ideology?

As early as 1947, Wright was determined to journey to Africa. On September 16 of that year he wrote in his journal, "I must see Africa. If this winter I can write this book that is in me, then I shall go to see that place and I say here and now that I shall write the only book about Africa that will be written in my time" (Journal 63). The journey did not take place until the spring of 1953, when, with an advance from Harper's, Wright boarded a ship in Liverpool bound for the Gold Coast. It was not his first visit to what is now termed the Third World. In addition to a vacation in Mexico in 1940, Wright had spent several months in Argentina in 1949–50 making the film version of *Native Son* (Fabre, *Unfinished* 338–47). During this sojourn he visited Haiti, making notes for a travel journal he planned to write. At that time he proposed working with UNESCO, which had pledged to publish information on the colored peoples of the world. Wright's services were declined because of his political past and his ignorance of the language.

This background is interesting in the context of the first chapter of *Black Power*, where the trip to Africa is proposed by Dorothy Padmore, in the course of an idle Easter Sunday afternoon. As they stir sugar into their coffee, Mrs. Padmore asks Wright, "Now that your desk is clear, why don't you go to Africa?" (3). He seems stunned: "The idea was so remote to my mind and mood that I gaped at her a moment before answering. '*Africa*? . . . ' " (3). The reader recalls that Wright was a close friend of George Padmore, whom in the text he only identifies as "West Indian author and journalist." Padmore was also an advisor to Kwame Nkrumah, soon to be head of the first independent African nation, Ghana. Any friend of Padmore's would not find the idea of a visit to Africa remote. Why conceal the fact that he had long planned to visit Africa? Or that he was passionately interested in the many nationalist movements throughout the continent? The fiction continues: " 'Africa!' I repeated the word to myself, then paused as something strange and disturbing stirred slowly in the depths of me. I am African! I'm of African descent. . . . Yet I'd never seen Africa; I'd never really known any Africans. I'd hardly ever thought of Africa" (3).

In fact the opposite was true. In 1947 Jean Paul Sartre introduced Wright to Léopold Senghor and Alioune Diop. And at Diop's request Wright agreed to become a sponsor for the journal *Présence Africaine*. In *The World of Richard Wright* Michel Fabre discusses in detail Wright's role in the journal, which included fund-raising

(Fabre 192–213). Wright's concealing (transparently) his familiarity with the Gold Coast sets the stage for *Black Power*'s two very different narratives; one would require the "objectivity" of anthropology and the other would permit the subjectivity of autobiography. He would write a timely report on the birth of this African nation *and* he would recount his very personal reactions to the ancestral homeland. The juxtaposition of the two narratives makes *Black Power* one of Wright's most dynamic works. It shares with Stein's *Everybody's Autobiography* the need to acknowledge an original, if problematic, relationship to this home and simultaneously demonstrate the extent to which one has moved beyond it.

The dual quality of the text is apparent from its opening pages. As Dorothy Padmore responds to his questions on the political situation in the Gold Coast, Wright mulls over what being of African descent has meant to him: "Phrases from my childhood rang in my memory: one-half Negro, one-quarter Negro, one-eighth Negro. . . . In thirty-eight of the forty-eight states of the American Federal Union, marriage between a white person and a person of African descent was a criminal offense" (5). As he recalls this dimension of racist America, he is reminded of its flip side; African-American friends would insist that Africans were a civilized people when Europeans were still cave dwellers or that they possessed a special genius for music and dance. Wright, "being either uninterested or unable to accept such arguments, . . . remained silent" (5). Between Dorothy Padmore's clipped descriptions of Nkrumah's political movement, Wright consults the *Encyclopaedia Britannica.* The Gold Coast entry contained only three paragraphs on its people. This of course fuels his determination: "I wanted to see the crumbling slave castles where my ancestors had lain panting in hot despair. The more I thought of it, the more excited I became, and yet I could not rid myself of a vague sense of disquiet" (6). The juxtaposition of an encyclopedia entry and "my ancestors panting in hot despair" perfectly illustrates the tension between the two genres in *Black Power.* Wright's *Black Power* extends Countee Cullen's famous query "What is Africa to me?" to include "What does being *African* mean . . . ?" (4). Is Africanness constituted culturally or biologically? And finally would he, an African-American expatriate writer, find a piece to the puzzle of his own identity?

Just as Stein's methodology in *Everybody's Autobiography* works to destabilize the meaning of "autobiography" and "identity," Wright demonstrates the extent to which "history," "accurate information," or his own African ancestry are inadequate resources on the Gold Coast. Before he arrived in the port town of Takoradi on June 16, 1953, Wright had done his homework. As he would do for *Pagan Spain,* Wright consulted a number of studies: *Capitalism and Slavery* by Eric Williams; *A History of the Gold Coast* by W. E. F. Ward; *Ashanti* by R. S. Rattray; *Social Survey Sekondi-Takoradi* by K. A. Busia; *The Sacred State of the Akan* by Eva Meyerowitz and *The Akan Doctrine of God* by J. B. Danquah. While in Accra Wright met and interviewed Dr. Busia and Dr. Danquah, both members of the party in opposition to Nkrumah and both educated in Great Britain. As we will see, the experts and their information often thwarted his understanding and demonstrate that he is not getting the point.

Wright incorporates a special kind of authorization, illustrated by a letter of introduction that appears at the beginning of the text. In the letter, Kwame Nkrumah states that he has known Richard Wright for many years and believes him well qualified to visit the Gold Coast in preparation for a book on his observations. In this context the letter, intended to expedite the formalities of obtaining a visa, becomes an evocation of the letters of introduction at the beginning of slave narratives. Such letters served to authenticate the slave's narrative and underscored the former slave's dependence on the white writer to make his or her story known. By using Nkrumah's letter in this way, Wright amends this formula characteristic of a quintessential American genre; he recalls this literary practice, to signal, as in his revision of Irving and Hemingway, a new chapter in American literary history. This gesture places *Black Power* squarely within the American literary tradition, born of American slavery, and announces Wright's African *and* non-African origins. Wright acknowledges his dependence on Nkrumah for authentication and simultaneously registers his relationship to Africa via slavery, and his distance from it via the need for Nkrumah's nod of approval. On some level, *Black Power* can best be understood through this paradigm. That Wright should refer to the slave narrative is appropriate because African slavery is the starting point of his journey.

For Wright, Eric Williams's Marxist history of the slave trade was the least problematic source. Once in the Gold Coast, however, the other authoritative sources are often challenged by Wright's informants or by his experience. For example, when Wright cites the anthropologist R. S. Rattray's work in conversation with a chief, he dismisses its validity," Oh, Rattray . . . We didn't tell him *everything*. We told him *some* things. But we *never* tell *anybody* *everything* . . . " (290). But where he would be suspicious of the chief's denial of Rattray's authority here, in a similar situation, he finds the discrepancy between his British sources and the Gold Coast reality an inevitable feature of a colonial system. For just as Nkrumah's program for political reform threatened to paralyze the country's economy, a British expert, briefing a group of civil servants in London, made this assessment: "The Gold Coast is a kind of colonial Eden. You'll find the natives gentle, satisfied and deeply grateful for what we've done for them" (119). These episodes illustrate Wright's uncertain position; on the one hand he had to rely on British sources to make sense of what he saw; at the same time, the evidence frequently argued that his sources were not wholly reliable.

During Wright's visit to Mampong in the heart of the Ashanti region, one of the king's grandsons was assigned to escort him around. The young man was a photographer whom Wright had met in London. When Wright began to probe into the rituals and customs of the Ashanti, his guide became evasive. Asked about the role of the three young boys in the king's entourage, the photographer replied, "They just follow him" (279). When the Queen Mother of the household rose to speak, Wright noticed that one of her servants turned over her stool, a sacred icon in the Ashanti religion. Wright asked about this, "Oh, that . . . It just fell over; that's all" (281). Wright fumes: "He had again evaded telling me the truth, and yet I held under my arm a volume by a British anthropologist, which explained the turning over of the stool" (281). The British anthropologist is

R. S. Rattray, whom, curiously, Wright does not name at this moment. Exasperated, Wright donned his aggressive investigative reporter's hat. In the Queen Mother's compound, Wright observed a number of men and women wandering around who were not introduced. Wright barraged his guide with questions:

"Who are these people? Are they guests of the Queen Mother?"
"Oh, no." "Are they friends?" "No." "Are they servants?" "Well, no . . . "
"Are they paid?" "Well, no; we don't pay them." "But they work for her?"
"Yes." "Can they leave if they want to?" "They'd never want to leave."
"Are they slaves?" (281–82)

After several minutes of silence, the photographer stated the facts: these people would not want to leave, they were housed, clothed, fed, and treated as members of the family. Wright persisted, "But other people would call them slaves, wouldn't they?" (282). The guide grudgingly agreed to this but insisted that the word "slave" did not accurately describe their position. Wright concluded, "It was slavery all right; . . . not quite the Mississippi kind; it fitted in with their customs, beliefs. There was no lynching. . . . I stared at the slaves. I tried to swallow and I could not" (282).

At this moment, a purely anthropological narrative would dictate that Wright include a description of slavery according to his expert, R. S. Rattray. But Wright postpones this for several pages and only includes Rattray's explanation of Ashanti slavery to elucidate another context. And not surprisingly it corroborates what his guide had told him: "It was custom in Ashanti for male members of a clan to purchase female slaves by whom they had children. . . . These persons lived and grew up with the family and were treated by them very much as members of that family, and . . . looked upon the master's home as their domicile" (Rattray 43).

This is Wright's incorporation of Rattray's definition: "Slaves occupy a strange and privileged relationship with African families. The offspring of masters and slaves are considered as a legitimate part of the family. If the family line is threatened with extinction, a slave can and has been elevated to the head of the family" (306). Wright understood the system of Ashanti slavery particularly as it differed from "the Mississippi kind." And it is also clear from the text that he had read Rattray before he visited Mampong.

During his visit to the Queen Mother's compound, Wright knew that some of its residents would be slaves. So his decision to exclude Rattray's definition at this crucial moment, and having established that his guide was deceptive, permitted his own interpretation to take precedence. Wright's very personal response, "It was slavery all right; . . . not quite the Mississippi kind," places the focus of this encounter not on the system of Ashanti slavery but on the impact of American slavery on Richard Wright. In the anthropological narrative with which this episode begins, Wright would have questioned forms of slavery in general terms. But unlike the dispassionate British anthropologist or the very passionate Ashanti guide, Wright could not qualify his response any more than "not quite the Mississippi kind." Wright's uneasy position between the black African and the white Westerner recurs throughout *Black Power*.

Just as Gertrude Stein had purposefully sabotaged the possibility of "autobiography," in *Everybody's Autobiography*, *Black Power* exposes the limits of Richard Wright's accessibility to "Africa." What exactly is the content of the "African" part of African American? Does it suggest a biological, cultural, or political bond? Richard Wright struggled with these questions in every encounter because at its core, *Black Power* is about Wright's quest to come to terms with the history that produced the phenomenon of Richard Wright. In their quest for clarity on the subject of identity and origins, our writers begin at the beginning, that is, with the inordinate power of nouns to define.

Stein's abhorrence of nouns is well known. Indeed, among her most important contributions to American literature are the many ways in which she found to dislodge the sign and signified, pointing to their conventional and arbitrary relationship. Throughout the narrative of her American journey, Stein takes every opportunity to point out the indeterminate relationship between the sign and signified. Shortly after her arrival in New York, she noticed, "an electric sign moving around a building and it said Gertrude Stein has come"

(175). This aspect of celebrity gave her the "shock of recognition and non-recognition. It is one of the things most worrying in the subject of identity" (175). Stein invokes Aristotle to remind us that her own aesthetics developed in opposition to the *Poetics*. The "non-recognition" she adds to this formula is key to her fundamental problem with identity. What does that name in lights have to do with Gertrude Stein, the woman or the artist? It parallels the problem Wright encountered in the Gold Coast; what did his dark skin have to do with that world? Or how did the white world "epidermalize Being?" (Johnson 52).

For Stein, intrinsic to the proper noun was the problem of recognition. The pernicious aspect of recognition was external expectation because it interfered with creativity. Stein might lose interest in her work if, by popular demand, she were to produce only sequels to Alice's autobiography. In the second chapter of *Everybody's Autobiography*, Stein confessed, "All this time I did no writing. I had written and was writing nothing" (64). Attempts to reassure herself failed: "I began to worry about identity. I had always been I because I had words that had to be written inside me and now any word I had inside could be spoken it did not need to be written. I am I because my little dog knows me. But was I I when I had no written word inside me. It was very bothersome . . . I was not doing any writing" (64).

On the lecture circuit (the occasion for the electric light hoopla), Stein coped with the problem of recognition by never permitting herself to be introduced. An introduction prolonged the anxiety of beginning her talk and heightened the audience's expectation. And as she observed, "it was silly everybody knew who I was if not why did they come" (177).

The idea that names are linked to an individual's identity is subverted throughout *Everybody's Autobiography*: "anybody nowadays can call anybody any name they like" (10). The Chinese servants she employed often used borrowed or falsified identity papers; nonetheless, "they seem to be there or not there as well with any name" (10). Similarly Stein notes that Picasso's father's name was Ruiz and his mother's name was Picasso. That he chose the name which bears his legendary achievement erodes the definitive quality of the proper noun as does the very conventional way in which she was named: "When any of us were named we were named after some one who is already dead . . . so there was a grandmother she was dead and her name not an easy one began with G so my mother preferred it should be an easy one so they named me Gertrude Stein" (115). What if her grandmother's name had begun with an A?

Stein was grateful for recognition not of her name but of the literary achievements attached to it. This recognition is illustrated in her encounters with three African Americans, which punctuate the beginning and the conclusion of her tour. On the day that *Portraits and Prayers* came out, Stein went for a walk. A young black woman recognizing her from the photograph on the cover of the book displayed in a store window, looked at her, pointed to the copy of the book, and then smiled (8). When Stein first arrived in New York an elderly black man introduced himself as the music teacher of one performer in *Four Saints in Three Acts*. Stein does not recall the man's name for just as her own name was less important than her work, the names of those who expressed genuine appreciation of her work were beside the point.

This point is underscored in the selection of photographs included in the text. The photos are thank-you notes to the people, places, and pets who made the narrative possible. These photos, taken by Carl Van Vechten for *Everybody's Autobiography*, include one of Stein and the dogs, one of Alice Toklas, and one of Lucy Church in Bilignin. One pictures William Rogers, the GI Gertrude and Alice adopted during World War I who later became instrumental in their decision to make the trip back to the States. There is another photo of Stein surrounded by students (she is not visible) at William and Mary and a portrait of her wearing the dress in which she delivered her lectures. Finally, there is a photograph of black Americans Edward Matthews, who played the role of St. Ignatius, and Beatrice Robinson-Wayne, who played the role of St. Teresa, from the opera *Four Saints in Three Acts*. Significantly there are no photographs of her name in lights or of her shaking hands with the First Lady. Toward the end of the journey, Robinson-Wayne telephoned Stein: "When I said who is it, a voice answered Saint

Theresa, and that was my farewell to America, it was she . . . and she was Saint Theresa for herself and for us" (195).

Where Stein challenged the assumption that a proper name could adequately express one's identity, she insisted that some nouns better expressed group identity than others. Carl Van Vechten had organized a party of several black intellectuals in her honor. She observed that African Americans preferred the term "colored" to "Negro." "I dislike it when instead of saying Jew they say Hebrew or Israelite or Semite, I do not like it and why should a Negro want to be called colored" (200). "Colored" denies the group's integrity, an integrity she felt was preserved by the name "Negro." So even as she would argue that a noun was a "stupid thing," she concludes that both "Jew" and "Negro" were "nice strong solid names and so let us keep them" (200). Stein's defense of "Negro" and "Jew" is an assertive, offensive strategy that argues for a reappropriation of a name that in a hostile mouth is a curse. Perhaps the most relevant example here is African Americans' appropriation of "nigger" to express solidarity with and affection for friends and family members. Stein might have approved of this; the problem, however, is that outside this group, it retains the resonance of its ugly history, as do other racial slurs. But here Stein argues that "meaning" is conferred and the victims of racial slurs have always known this. One must reject the negative connotation and reappropriate the term. This is an ongoing project in African-American communities; since the 1960s, the term "black" has changed dramatically. Richard Wright's *Black Power* anticipates the ways in which "black" and "blackness" were redefined by the Civil Rights movement. The phenotypical difference, upon which the fiction of racial difference was developed and sustained, is at the center of *Black Power*. Wright's relationship to the African continent was, as he put it, illustrated "by the color of my skin." This single feature of Richard Wright's identity raised the most important questions in the text.

Within an hour of his arrival at the port in Takoradi, Wright was asked by a young African clerk if he knew from what part of Africa his ancestors had come. The question surprised him. Wright replied, "Well, . . . you know, you fellows who sold us and the white men who bought us didn't keep any records" (35). Slavery is on Wright's mind throughout his stay in Africa not simply because his grandfather had been born an American slave but because it represented all that was wrong with traditional societies. Even in the best context, it collided with one of Wright's most revered values: political, economic, intellectual, and artistic freedom.

In another interview, Wright again takes up the question of his ancestors and slavery. A British missionary, Lloyd Shirer, helped Wright interview an African from a remote northern territory. Wright described him as "about forty" and "jet black." Shirer introduced Wright as an American who had come to learn about the land of his ancestors. Wright asks about the man's religious beliefs and learns that he observes tribal rituals and customs. Wright asks if he has ever thought of going to America: "Oh, no, sar! Never! . . . I couldn't leave the land of my ancestors" (193). Wright then asks the big question: "What . . . happened to the millions of your black brothers who were sold into slavery and shipped to America?" (194). Thoughtful for a moment, the man supposed that these men and women had been punished. Had they appealed to their ancestors, they might have been saved. Wright asks, "You can see from the color of my skin that I am of African descent. Now, after all these years, why do you think I've come back to the land of my ancestors? Do you think that they called me back for some reason?" (194). The man became thoughtful and replied, "It's hard to tell sar, . . . I'm afraid, sar, that your ancestors do not know you now" (195). Wright's thoughts return to slavery and his informant's belief in "dreams dreamed with the eyes wide open" (196).

Another encounter upon which skin color is pivotal occurs when Wright wanders into a funeral. On one of his first ventures into the city, the sound of beating drums led him to a compound where a group of people were dancing. He paused, "Ought I go in? They were black and so was I. But my clothes were different from theirs; they would know me for a stranger" (125). Wright asked a young man permission to enter, and the youth agreed to escort him. Wright asked, "Why are they dancing?" The young man explained that a girl had just died. Wright stared at the dancers and repeated his question, to which he was given the same reply. Again before leaving, he restated the question and received the same answer. Wright wandered out thinking, "I had understood nothing. I was black and they were black, but my blackness did not help me" (127).

Soon after this episode, Wright found himself at the funeral of a chief. The scene was organized chaos, replete with "half-nude women" in raffia skirts, whose faces were streaked with white paint. Men fired guns into the air and beat drums, as the coffin jerked erratically from one direction to another: "I had understood nothing, nothing . . . I looked closer and saw that the faces of the women and children were marked with a reddish paint on the left cheek. . . . My mind reeled at the newness and strangeness of it. Had my ancestors acted like that? And why?" (130). This question expresses the distance between himself and those ancestors, but it also echoes part of white America's racist ideology that assumes that just beneath the thin veneer of a Westernized surface, most African Americans are spitting distance from the "jungle." Wright's apparent obtuseness counters this assumption; donning the mask of the mystified Westerner enables him to mark the distance (figured through confusion even when events are explained to him) from that world. But just as these encounters underscore Wright's alienation from his African origins, there are other incidents that complicate this question.

Soon after Wright arrived, Nkrumah took him on a tour of Accra. As the crowd hailed Nkrumah with shouts of "Kwame! Free-dooom!" Wright's attention was riveted to the exuberant dance of the women. Suddenly he realized: "I'd seen these same snakelike, veering dances before . . . Where? Oh, God, yes; in America, in store front churches, in Holy Roller Tabernacles . . . on the plantations of the Deep South" (56). Before coming to the Gold Coast, Wright believed only that he would not feel at home in a culture so removed from his own. To witness elements of African America in far-off Accra was disturbing; it challenged his belief that "racial qualities were but myths of prejudiced minds" (57). But Wright is more perplexed by its implications for his identity. If such dancing were a racial trait, surviving centuries of oppression and assimilation in America, why had it never manifested itself in him? "How much am I a part of this? How much was I part of it when I saw it in America? . . . Why that peculiar, awkward restraint when *I* tried to dance or sing? . . . Had I denied all this in me? . . . Why had my hands and feet, all my life, failed to keep time? . . . I had wanted to, because it had always been part of my environment, *but I had never been able to*!" (58). The remarkable extremes registered in Wright's experience in *Black Power* suggest, despite or because of the explorer's persona, the difficulty of the task to which he is committed. In the space of an hour he might be reminded of something from his Mississippi boyhood, or he might feel as though he has been dropped down on another planet.

For both Stein and Wright the encounter with origins, real or imputed, raised the question of the distance between themselves and their "homes." In both narratives, the authors point to the distance between themselves and their origins through their commitment to the radically New in politics and poetics. In *Black Power,* Wright's struggle to come to terms with the traditional dimensions of life in the Gold Coast echoes his resistance to the religious and racial orthodoxies with which he was raised. Even as Stein celebrates the modern in American architecture, air travel, and cinema, she remains as critical of those features of American life that resist radical innovation.

In a paradox with which she was at home, Stein argues that America's modernity is linked to its oldest feature: the natural landscape. In *The Geographical History of America,* Stein writes, "Scenery has no beginning middle and ending" (218). The American landscape incorporated the atemporal quality she believed characterized a masterpiece. And by claiming certain aspects of it, she accounts for the timeless quality of her work and affirms her identity as an American writer. In the United States, Stein made her first journey by air, which gave her a new perspective on physical reality. From the great distance Stein saw in the landscape the source of modernist painting. In *Picasso* Stein reiterated this point: "When I was in America I for the first time traveled pretty much all the time in an airplane and when I looked at the earth I saw all the lines of cubism made at a time when not any painter had ever gone up in an airplane. I saw there on the earth the mingling lines of Picasso, coming and going, developing and destroying themselves, I saw the simple solutions of Braque, I saw the wandering lines of Masson, yes I saw and once more I knew that a creator is contemporary" (Stein 50). In *Everybody's Autobiography*, Stein's enthusiasm is not for the landscape but for the way that physical reality illuminated a man-made design: "I never can stop having pleasure in the way the ruled lines separate one state from another . . . it always gives me a shock of pleasure the American map . . . compare it to any other with the way they go all over nothing neat and clean like the maps of America" (192). The relationship between the continent and the map is analogous to the relationship between the imagination and its expression in painting or in literature. From the air, Stein decides: "That is what I like about America it is interesting even if there is no water in the ocean of it" (294). The American continent illustrated the chaos of imagination and its "clear," "clean," and "neat" expression.

In American architecture too Stein saw the modernist dimension of the national character. When she left the United States in 1904, the Flatiron building was the tallest in New York City. Thirty years later, she notes that the newer buildings had no cornices, "and that is right because why end anything" (202). Stein was intrigued by Rockefeller Center, under construction during her stay. It was built "so quietly so thinly and so rapidly" that it gave her the impression of "something that does make existence a non-existent real thing" (202). Stein's meaning here is elaborated in her comments on Picasso's cubism.

In a 1938 essay, Stein located the source of Picasso's cubism in the juxtaposition of Spanish landscape and Spanish architecture. In France and Italy, she argued, architecture followed the lines of the natural surroundings. But in Spain, architecture developed in opposition to those features. Stein argues that cubism releases the spirit of the twentieth century, where "nothing is in agreement, neither the round with the cube, neither the landscape with the houses" (Stein 23–24). She extends this observation of Spain to include America and herself. Only the truly modern artist, uninterested in verisimilitude or continuity, could express existence as a "non-existent real thing." And for Stein, the Rockefeller building, imbued with this quality, was a work of twentieth-century art.

There is another aspect of Picasso's cubism that Stein neglects to consider, and yet it illuminates much about his work and her own. Michael North argues that both Stein's and Picasso's (indeed all of the Moderns') innovations were catalyzed by African and/or African-American art forms. To make of existence "a non-existent real thing" suggests to me an extreme distancing that the African mask (as Picasso employed it) or the African-American voice as Stein assumed it, could pull off. "In each case, in painting and in literature, the step away from conventional verisimilitude into abstraction is accomplished by a figurative change of race" (North 61). To make it new had to mean a break with the past, with convention. The African and African-American figure/voice facilitated this break, extended the rupture that expatriation initiated. We might also wonder how much that Spanish landscape, its architecture, and its aesthetics had been shaped, as was the United States, by centuries of the presence of the African Other on its soil. This feature was, as we have seen, key to Wright's interest in Spain.

Gertrude Stein was at home with American architecture, technological innovations, and natural settings because they reflected her aesthetics. But some encounters reminded her of the disturbing features of American life. College students were conservative and unimaginative. At the University of Virginia she challenged them, "What was the use of being young if they have the same opinions as all of them who were eighty or a hundred" (249). This echoes a key sentence in *The Geographical History of America*: "What is the use of being a boy if you are going to grow up to be a man." Youthful curiosity and imagination are opposed to a lack of either in the mature adult. Stein's provocation eventually netted her a two-week teaching position at the University of Chicago. She was incensed that none of the curriculum's great books were written in English. Consequently, the University invited her to give a seminar with students from every discipline. After one particularly animated discussion, the professor remarked on the way the students had responded. Stein explained: " 'You see why they talk to me is that I am like them I do not know the answer, you say you do not know but you do . . . if you did not know the answer you could not spend your life in teaching but I I really do not know . . . whether there is a question let alone having an answer for a question' " (213). Answers, like utopias and governments, shut down imagination and curiosity.

At Wesleyan College, Stein asks why American men are so devoted to financial success when 80 percent would do no better than break even. At the height of the Great Depression, this was a relevant question. She wonders why "they do not keep on being interested in the things that interested them when they were college men" (239). Even as she criticizes this quality, she is not immune to its interference in her own personality. Early in *Everybody's Autobiography*, she admits that she had subscribed to the "good American doctrine" that encourages enterprise. But failure is inevitable; this is true in every country, "only in America there has not been the habit of recognizing it" (65). The business of America may well be business, but for Stein this ethos produced a stifling conformity that stripped one of independence and originality. After World War II, Stein returned to this issue in her most radically political novel, *Brewsie and Willie*.

On the conservative values in American life, Richard Wright agreed with Stein's assessment. Of course both Stein and Wright, in career choice, in marriage, in what they would write about and why, in all that mattered most to each of them, had had to walk away from the well-worn paths. In *Black Power*, Wright encounters modern features in a largely traditional society, and his responses to these are mixed.

One afternoon, frustrated by the government's reluctance to help him tour the Gold Coast, Wright climbed into a taxi and told the driver to take him to a village. When they arrived, the driver urged Wright to find the chief and introduce himself. Wright strode into the village and was stopped by a friendly young man who spoke English. Wright's guide was an electrician who had been educated in a missionary school. Wright barraged him with questions on a broad range of subjects. As he observed the women pounding vegetables into the national dish, *fufu*, Wright turned to his guide and said, "Now look—you are an electrician. Why don't you invent a machine to pound that stuff" (146). The entire village laughed, but Wright persisted; Americans make bread with machines. As they stroll though the village, Wright wonders, "I was assuming that these people had to be pulled out of this life, out of these conditions of poverty, had to become literate and eventually industrialized. But why? Was not the desire for this mostly on *my* part rather than *theirs*? I was literate, Western, disinherited, and industrialized and I felt each day the pain and anxiety of it" (147; Wright's emphasis).

Wright's stake in the Gold Coast's political and social revolution was very personal: "there was the element of sheer pride in my wanting them to be different. With what godlikeness we all thought of the lives of others!" (148). As in the example of the *fufu*-pounding machine, Wright is like a visitor from the future who has come with a message for his ancestors. This analogy is also illustrated in the following dialogue between Wright and the electrician:

"Do you think somebody in America would give me a scholarship, sar?"
"Perhaps; but you have schools here."
"But I want to go to America, sar."
"What makes you think they give scholarships in America?"
"They're rich, sar."
"I was born there and nobody ever gave me one."
"But you are rich, sar; aren't you?"
"No. I'm not. I was born as poor or maybe poorer than you are now . . . I'm not rich."
"But you went to university, sar?"
"No."
"Then how did you become a writer, sar?"
"Because I wanted to be a writer. . . . you can study right here in Labadi and be anything you want to . . . ' " (144)

This exchange illustrates the extent to which Wright sees himself in the young man and, by extension, his bond to this very foreign place. Even Wright's most hostile critics have to concede that most white visitors to the Gold Coast did not find themselves identifying with its youth. It also illustrates Wright's belief in the transportability of Western values. The complexity of Wright's position on Western civilization is further illustrated in encounters with two African chiefs.

In his closing remarks to Nkrumah, Wright argued that the progress of the nation depended on the removal of the chiefs. The chief preserved beliefs and traditions that were antithetical to the modern world. Yet on his trip into the interior, Wright met two chiefs who elicited very different responses from him. The first greeted him warmly and invited him in to drink. Wright's manners were impeccable; he respectfully addressed the chief as "Nana," offered a flawless libation, and cleverly answered a riddle. The chief took Wright's arm and led him to a place where in the distance sat a black box. The chief asked Wright what he saw, and after a few incorrect guesses, the old man reported that the box contained his private army; he was protected by magical bees. Wright politely took his leave, adding, "And it was more than clear now why Nkrumah had to get rid of these old chiefs" (253).

Wright's encounter with another chief, however, reveals the contradiction in his own mind on the prospects of a Westernized African future. The elder man describes the chief's role in a tribal society. The chief wonders how his people will make the leap into the modern world, "They cannot grasp politics. Yet, history is making severe demands upon us and we are not prepared" (287). He asks Wright, an African American who has made the transition, for his opinion. Wright admits that despite appearances, African Americans had not achieved an ideal life in American society. Contrary to what he had suggested to the electrician, Wright argues that industrialization is not a panacea, "Machines are wonderful things; . . . but remember that they cannot tell you how to live" (288). Wright then adds, "You men of Africa must be able to tell the West something about how to live" (288). Wright's interview with this chief, a man who symbolized everything he thought wrong with African society, illuminated his own abiding ambivalence toward the West.

In Africa and Asia, Wright had difficulty reconciling traditional religious beliefs with efforts to implement modern versions of democracy and individualism. This is illustrated in a discussion of the Gold Coast's history with the electrician from Labadi. Wright asks, "Did the missionaries ever tell you to dedicate your life to free-ing your country?" They had not. "But they taught you to read didn't they? . . . And after they taught you to read, you read didn't you? And when you read, you found out that the British had taken your country? Is that it?" (148). The youth's response is vague, "I think so, sar." Wright resumes: "But the reading they [the missionaries] taught you, you used it to learn about freedom didn't you?" (149). The young man understood Wright's point and stated that someday his country would be free. It is clear that he did not make the con-nection between theory and practice. Wright wonders whether Chris-tianity or the indigenous religious traditions had done the African the most harm. That the two continued to coexist would only make the passage into the modern world that much more difficult.

Reconciling political activism and traditional religious practices should not have been difficult to imagine; by 1953, there were recent and dramatic examples of such alliances. Gandhi had catalyzed mil-lions into action with what he described as "satyagraha," that is, "soul force," itself a conflation of a traditional Hindu concept, with Henry David Thoreau's more modern civil disobedience. The combi-nation proved a formidable opponent to British rule. And Indian in-dependence in 1947 contributed much to the events Wright had come to witness in the Gold Coast. Indeed via Reverend Martin Luther King Jr., Gandhi had inspired the American Civil Rights movement. What was it about the blend of religion and politics that so nettled Richard Wright? Several incidents in *Black Power* are suggestive.

For *Black Power*, Wright consulted three books on the Akan reli-gion. His summary of Eva Meyerowitz's *The Sacred State of the Akan* is interesting because, like the discussion of slavery, Wright's use of it is revealing. When he met the King of the Ashanti, he could have included Meyerowitz's discussion of the Akan concept of kingship. Instead, on three separate occasions during this passage, Wright de-nies any personal adherence to Akan beliefs. On the cosmic origins of the human family, Wright states, "Now, I don't believe any of this, but I see nothing barbarous in it" (335). After paraphrasing the

complex reasons for matrilineal descent he adds, "I still do not believe a single word of all of this, yet I do not endorse the killing of a
single flea if that flea happened to believe it" (336). He describes the
elaborate burial rites for kings and concludes: "All of this seems
bizarre to me; I can't conceive of myself ever believing any of it; but,
still, I don't agree that people who do believe in such ought to be de-
clared biologically inferior!" (336–37). This compulsion to clarify
his own position might make sense if Wright had been the author of
the book he discusses, and the awkward prose further suggests that
he is fumbling. These three denials upstage the entire exposition.
Beyond the obvious fact that he does protest too much lies a more
important implication; Wright felt that his readers would assume
that he would or should share these beliefs. As an African American,
Wright is struggling against the idea of biological determinacy and
innate inferiority, the cap- and cornerstones of American racist
ideology. Evidence that this wholly discredited idea retains its hold
on the American psyche was apparent in the 1994 publication and
popularity of Richard Herrnstein's *Bell Curve: Intelligence and Class
Structure in American Life*.

Wright realized that the two European sources on the religious
beliefs of the Akan were insufficient, so he consulted *The Akan Doctrine of God* by the African scholar, J. B. Danquah. But Wright does
not compare Danquah's work with that of Rattray or Meyerowitz. Instead he confesses that he is not an empathetic reader of metaphysics. But in terms of Danquah's project, to clarify the tenets of
Akan religion, empathy is not important; *The Akan Doctrine of God*
is not an exhortation to the faithless. Wright claims that the text
"smacks of an unconscious apology, Danquah assumes that Christianity is believed superior and that the devotees of that religion are
too filled with racial prejudice to acknowledge that the African religion is just as good" (215). This is true, inasmuch as part of Danquah's task was to correct the misrepresentation of the Akan
religion. But in his criticism of Rattray and Westermann, Danquah
does not apologize for the Akan religious tradition.

The Europeans' racial prejudice is far less an issue for Danquah
than it is for Wright. It is the fact of their "Westernness" that seems

to blind Rattray and Westermann. Of Rattray, Danquah wrote: "But, probably being against the grain in the mind of a Christian, Rattray could not bring himself to comprehend what was the most obvious" (7). Of the aptly named Westermann, Danquah argues that his vision of African religion was clouded by "a nebulous tradition which, for centuries, had elected to look upon the African as a being with a 'mind' the direct opposite of Europe" (16–17). As such, it was impossible for him to concede to the Akan a highly developed, complex, and subtle religious tradition without European intervention.

Wright's first exchange with Danquah was telling. When Wright reported that he had been in the country about two months, Danquah said, "Stay longer and you'll *feel* your race" (218). Wright admits, "I liked the man, but not as a Negro or African; I liked his directness, his willingness to be open. Yet, I knew that I'd never feel an identification with Africans on a 'racial' basis" (219). During Wright's meeting with Danquah, very little of their discussion addressed the text or the Akan religious practices. When Wright finally raised the subject of religion, it was to ask Danquah how he could be both a Christian and observe his native religion. This question illuminates one of Wright's central concerns: the paradox of being both of African descent and a Westerner. Wright's dissatisfaction with Danquah's responses is tied to the African's inability to provide him with answers to questions raised by his own identity.

If clarity on the religious traditions was difficult for Wright, reconciling its practice with building a modern state would be almost impossible. Wright interviewed Dr. Kofi Busia, a faculty member at Achimota University and author of *Social Survey Sekondi-Takoradi*. This study addresses the impact of urbanization on tribal life, and Wright saw a parallel between it and the Chicago School of Sociology's work on the Great Migration. Busia argued that tribal customs, such as oath taking, were crucial to contemporary political life. Despite British claims, Busia insisted that traditional religious beliefs and practices were alive and well in the Gold Coast. Wright conceded that Busia's assessment of the situation was complex, and he wondered how a man with his training could continue to adhere to his tribal traditions. Wright asked if Nkrumah's nationalism would efface the old ways of life, and Busia replied, "The African will react in that matter just as all people react. . . . In the crucial moments of life, people fall back upon the deepest teachings of their lives; . . . in matters like politics, death, childbirth, etc., it's the teachings and beliefs of the tribe that all people—even those who are literate—turn to" (230). As an African, tribal traditions were important to him; as a Westerner, he knew that these traditions would be transformed in the process of modernization. Wright's interviews with Danquah and Busia were frustrating because, despite their Western training, these men were grounded in a reality that was inaccessible to Richard Wright.

Even though Wright had not expected to "feel his race," to feel solidarity based on biology, he assumed that these men might experience the alienation born of a "double consciousness." Wright's disaffection for Christianity is related to its role in his own early life and in American slavery. In *Black Boy* and elsewhere, Wright describes Christianity as a form of control and oppression. Wright knew the extent to which the objectionable features of religious traditions were universal. In *White Man, Listen!* he notes the similarity between an African taking an oath and French soldiers making the sign of the Cross before going into battle. Indeed part of the project in *Pagan Spain* is to demonstrate the extent to which Catholicism accommodates the "pagan," that is, irrational and superstitious practices, and this syncretism is part of what fascinates him about Spain and America. But in the Gold Coast, the emergence of a rich and productive creole culture seems remote; the presence of the Traditional is all too pervasive for Richard Wright.

After many meetings with men and woman from every segment of the Gold Coast's society, from the prime minister to the missionary's cook, Wright, as did Stein in *Paris France,* turned to an interpolated tale. And like the Helen Button episode, it is autobiographical. Wright introduces this imaginative sketch: "I'd now talked to enough educated Africans of the Gold Coast for there to emerge in my mind a dim portrait of an African character that the world knew little or nothing about" (231). As Wright weaves elements of his own life into the fiction, this dim portrait of men like Busia becomes a self-portrait. The story begins with a young African who is sent to a missionary school and then to study abroad. Western education alters his world; he returns home, forever alienated from the traditional society but committed to work for his nation's independence.

This fictive account of the African incorporates much of Wright's personal odyssey. The emphasis on individuality and a sense of personal destiny is evident throughout his work. Indeed the first crime in *Native Son* is the annihilation of Bigger's power to realize his individuality except through crime. For the African, religion becomes "mumbo jumbo."

The protagonist's critique of America is Wright's own. After the publication of *Native Son* had earned him critical acclaim and financial security, Wright was never free from racially motivated insults, even in "liberal" Greenwich Village. Indeed part of Wright's decision to leave the United States was the daily, petty expressions of racism: that he had to go to Harlem to get his hair cut, that he would be called "boy" by neighborhood shopkeepers, that in restaurants he would be served salted coffee if in the company of his Jewish American wife. And finally in the spring of 1947, white gangs began violent attacks on interracial couples (Fabre, *Unfinished* 312). On another occasion, Wright had an appointment to meet Sinclair Lewis at a hotel in downtown Manhattan. When he arrived, the doorman told him to use the servants' entry (Fabre, *Unfinished* 591, n.35).

Like his protagonist, Wright frequently stopped to hear speeches made by members of the Communist Party in Union Square and Washington Park. A fictional account of this appears in his first novel, *Lawd Today!* In the tale, Wright also refers to his experience with *Présence Africaine*; Wright abhorred French hostility toward their colonial subjects, which had become horrific during the Algerian War. Wright's portrait might have described Danquah's or Nkrumah's experience in the West; but neither African would register the sense of alienation from tribal society Wright imagines.

Still, however alien Wright found some features of African tribal life, however much he measured his distance from it, he could not fully endorse the Western way of life. The West had used him and myriad "expendable" Others to build its Great Traditions. Wright's position is evident in the dedication to *Black Power*: "TO THE UN-KNOWN AFRICAN who, because of this primal and poetic humanity was regarded by white men as a 'thing' to be bought, sold, and used as an instrument of production; and who alone in the forests of West Africa, created a vision of life so simple as to be terrifying, yet a vision that was irreducibly human."

Wright hated the poverty, illness, and illiteracy he found in the Gold Coast, which he believed were exacerbated by traditional beliefs. Through the interpolated tale he expressed an alienation that, in the Gold Coast, was his alone. As Amiri Baraka put it, "Africa is a foreign place. You are / as any other sad man here / american."

The individual is the locus of the tension Wright expresses between "traditional" and "modern." Richard Wright was not convinced that "individualism" could flourish in a traditional society. This conflict (religious training being just one of its features) is the dynamic at work in Robert Park's theory of the Marginal Man. At the same time, the isolation expressed above explicitly states the disadvantage of the American obsession with the autonomous self. Before leaving the United States definitively, Wright had purchased a home for his mother and Aunt Maggie and he continued to support them as long as they lived, which in the case of his mother, was until just a few months before his own death in November 1960. In addition to continued support of African-American writers such as James Baldwin, Ralph Ellison, Chester Himes, and Gwendolyn Brooks, Wright's generosity took other forms. Along with psychiatrist Frederic Wertham, he helped found a drop-in clinic for New York City's troubled black youth (Fabre, *Unfinished* 272). Wright never severed the ties to his family members or to the black American community, but he refused to be defined exclusively by his relationship to them. For Richard Wright individualism was one of the very few American rights that the heirs of the stolen sons and daughters of Africa could claim.

Even when Wright fails to see the possibility of individual expression within a tribal society or to appreciate the psychic need for ritual or custom in any society, his questions throughout *Black Power* grapple with and go beyond W. E. B. Du Bois's formulation of the problem of the twentieth century. Du Bois's "color-line" functions as both trope and complex reality by the time Wright visits the Gold Coast or when in 1955 he attends the Bandung Conference in Indonesia. Wright's questions and observations articulate the problems of a whole new world; things were, as Achebe eloquently observed, falling apart. Critics who fault Wright's impatience and disdain with life in the Gold Coast should recall that he was the one of very few black Americans at Bandung in 1955. His work in exile was devoted to making the emerging nations of Africa and Asia visible to the Western world. He was, like Stein, "violently devoted to the New," even when he could not imagine novelty emerging from a traditional world.

Richard Wright dedicated his collection of essays, *White Man, Listen!*, to "the Westernized and tragic elite of Asia, Africa and the West Indies." These people of color lived "on the clifflike margins of many cultures" and were, as was Wright, homeless. Whether we think of this as a kind of transcendent homelessness or as the marginality of modernity so familiar to both Wright and Stein, this dedication gets to the heart of their separate and mutual concerns. Marginality was both a blessing and a curse, and in the dialectic between the center and the periphery one finds the origins of modernity. Both writers saw this relationship as an intrinsic part of their creativity. Certainly the marginal's credentials borne by Wright opened doors, fueled his curiosity, and focused his energies on projects as apparently disparate as *Savage Holiday* and "Five Episodes from an Unfinished Novel." (*Savage Holiday* is a psychological thriller with an all-white cast, whereas the five episodes follow the exploits of young and disoriented Fishbelly Tucker, from *The Long Dream*, in Paris where he has come to escape certain death at the hands of the white sheriff back in Mississippi.) In that evocative phrase, "Brother Singulars, we are misplaced in a generation that knows not Joseph," Stein expresses the anguish of being excluded and marginalized. In *Everybody's Autobiography*, she returns to celebrate that very feature of her long and productive life.

Stein attributed her originality, in part, to having come from California, literally and figuratively on the American margin. During the lecture at William and Mary College, she affirmed this idea as she prodded the Virginians: "Somebody has to have an original feeling and it might be a Californian or a Virginian. It was a Californian because I was there from six to seventeen. . . . California and Virginia have at one time had a feeling that they were not part of just being American. . . . Richmond and San Francisco did not make anybody know what was American" (249). To explore the relationship between marginality and creativity, Stein returned to the place that had helped her to articulate this alienation, the African-American community.

Like the photographs that accompany *Everybody's Autobiography*, Gertrude Stein's America includes the African-American community. In addition to the intellectual elite at Van Vechten's party, Stein met with the all-black company who performed *Four Saints in Three Acts*. Virgil Thomson, who wrote the opera's music, took the idea for an all-black cast from a line in the first act, "Could a negro be be with a beard to see and to be" (448). When he told Stein of his plan she initially objected, saying that it was not what she had in mind. Still, she permitted him the final decision and never regretted it (Bridgman 181). Stein also met with the African-American "everybody." One rainy evening Stein and Toklas rode around Chicago with a couple of homicide detectives. When they entered an apartment in the black ghetto Stein asked each resident where he/she was from, as she did with anyone she met. The dwelling reminded her of the ones she had known in Baltimore, which then recalls the origins of "Melanctha."

Until very recently, Stein's relationship to African-American artists was rarely discussed. Yet her best-known work, "Melanctha," came out of her work as a medical student in Baltimore's black community. In that short story, Stein re-created the psychological anguish of her affair with May Bookstaver. That she chose the black community to express this episode suggests a range of possible meanings. Recall that Stein had already written this love triangle in *QED*, her first novel. Unsatisfied with the results, she tried again, making the white characters black and the autobiographical Adele a Dr. Jefferson Campbell. Stein's donning a black mask may have made it easier for her "to see the senses, even the body itself, as ruled by convention" (North 70). The shift of race also helped her to articulate the extent to which she experienced alienation at home. For Stein, the definitive power of skin color in the United States paralleled the definitive power of sexual identity. Despite the advantages of class and color, Stein, a Jewish woman and a lesbian, felt as excluded from American society as did members of the black community. This is evident in the context of the other two stories that make up *Three Lives*. She knew the German immigrant community more intimately than the African-American; Stein's autobiographical character, Miss Mathilda, has a marginal role in "The Good Anna." But the black community's exclusion from American society better represented the chasm she felt between herself and her peers.

Consider the 1909 quotation from Stein's notebook, "I believe in reality as Cezanne [*sic*] or Caliban believe in it." The relationship between Cézanne, Caliban, and Gertrude Stein, particularly in 1909, is key to our understanding of the modernist aesthetic and to modernity as well. North wonders that none of Stein's critics have ever addressed the implications of this trinity and poses these questions: "Is she claiming . . . that Cézanne introduces us to a reality as basic as that lived by Caliban, or that Caliban has as unsettling an effect on our notions of reality as Cézanne? "Melanctha" seems the first representation of this paradoxical reality, presided over as it was by Cézanne . . . and Caliban the freakishly distorted stereotype who mixes "strong black curses" with "the wide abandoned laughter that gives the broad glow of negro sunshine" (North 64). How are we to understand this mixture of aesthetic experimentation and racist crudity? These questions point to an important failing in Stein scholarship; one either deals with the aesthetics of *Three Lives* or dismisses her as a vulgar racist, and neither position helps us understand her relationship to Caliban.

A way into a more fruitful discussion may be to begin with Prospero. What Caliban does is remind us that "Prospero's narrative is not simply history, not simply the way things were, but a particular *version*" (Hulme 124). And as Houston Baker recalls, Caliban must respond to being possessed by both Prospero and his language

(Baker 54–60). As an American, Stein would have taken the side of the captive and colonized Caliban, particularly in the struggle to find an antitraditional aesthetic. Stein's masking her coming-out story through blackface parallels the ways in which black artists used racial stereotypes to disguise deeply subversive challenges to the status quo. Examples include Charles Chesnutt's *Conjure Woman,* Bert Williams's minstrel performances, and, as Houston Baker argues, Booker T. Washington's rhetorical strategies in *Up From Slavery* (Baker 29–30). Just as the distortion of black American dialect had alerted Stein to the discrepancy between speech and its representation, so too did the stereotypical "wide abandoned laughter that gives the broad glow of negro sunshine" point to the difference between mask and/or persona and human beings. Interesting too is Stein's use of this offensive phrase. Rose Johnson and James Herbert are defined, in part, by not having the "wide abandoned laughter" (59, 64). How could they, given the facts of their lives? The only character to possess this quality is the autobiographical character Jefferson Campbell (77, 96). More important, Stein understood the ways in which stereotypes work to alienate society's outcasts both from themselves and from the mainstream.

What is it that Caliban, Cézanne, and Stein share that enables her to make this assertion? I suggest it is an oppositional position to the orthodox gloss on reality. For Stein, Caliban is an important ancestor in that his refusal to accept reality is apparent in his speech, the cultural medium Prospero bestows upon him, in protoimperial arrogance. Caliban curses, counters, negates, and refuses Prospero's version; even though Caliban must now curse Prospero in his language, he discovers that he can use that medium to refute the conventions, forms, values both aesthetic and social, they transmit. For example, Stein's use of repetition renders phrases like "broad glow of negro sunshine" meaningless. At the same time, the circuitous and agonizingly painful repetitions with variation that convey Jeff and Melanctha's relationship compel the reader to share in their misery to such an extent that the stereotypes with which the story began are revealed to be the props they always were. The experience is like seeing the set of a Hollywood Western. From one angle it looks quite genuine. But when you've walked around a bit, you know where you are and where you are not. In both Cézanne and Stein, the innovative process enabled the discovery of the arbitrary relationship between a name/noun/stereotype and that to which it refers.

In Fort Worth, Texas, Stein attended a production of the play *Porgy*. She was impressed by the performance of the black man in the lead role. She argues that, for many black performers, "acting is not acting, but being" and "they can be what anything makes them and it does not make anything else of them because they are the thing they are then" (279). This quality she links to a lack of self-consciousness and a lack of "time sense." Is this the romantic racialism of the white patrons of the Harlem Renaissance who celebrated the African American as more "natural," as the twentieth-century version of the noble savage? Langston Hughes parodies the cult of the "natural" in the short stories "Rejuvenation through Joy" and "Slave on the Block" from *The Ways of White Folks*. This notion assumed that African ancestry endowed the American black with childlike spontaneity, a lack of sexual inhibition, and an innate gift for dance and song.

Gertrude Stein's assessment of the African American's talent for acting echoes her definition of genius: "a genius is some one who does not have to remember the two hundred years that everybody else has to remember" (121). "There must be a reality that has nothing to do with the passage of time and it is very hard for anyone to have that in them . . . I have it" (154). Key to artistic genius was the lack of a sense of time and self-consciousness which is how she describes the star of *Porgy*. Neither she nor the black artists she has defined as geniuses were without self-consciousness or a sense of time. Rather it was the ability to distance themselves or to disidentify with these constraining definitions (Caliban's refusal) that enabled the process of creativity. From 1619 to the present, black America's survival has depended on refusing white America's definition of it. This echoes Orlando Patterson's observation that "there is absolutely no evidence from the long and dismal annals of slavery to suggest that any group of slaves ever internalized the conception of degradation held by their masters" (97).

Stein invokes the sense of life lived at a distance to account for this genius, and African Americans were the best example of this alienation (the same psychological distance Wright attributed to his grandmother). Stein felt that her sexual identity and her Jewish origins had contributed to her unique perspective. These facts of her life functioned in the same way that living in California and in France had; they provided the marginality requisite for her creative work. On the other hand, being an outcast in your native land is painful and infuriating. So not only was a genius made by a nation in the process of forming itself, she made herself in opposition to a society that would contain its members in rigid definitions of race, ethnicity, or sexuality.

Stein made this point more directly by noting the way Native Americans were relegated to a subhuman category in American society. Stein and Toklas toured Yosemite National Park with an enthusiastic guide who boasted of the park's wild animals and Indians. Stein observes, "There were of course Indians there and they were proud of them but it was not interesting, after all Indians know more about not being wild when they are not wild than animals do" (287). In an extremely shrewd move Stein establishes the relationship between Native Americans and the elite Anglo-Americans who comprised the student body of Ivy League Colleges. At the Yale/Dartmouth football game, Stein notes that the movement of the players resembled an Indian dance: "Art is inevitable everybody is as their air and land is everybody is as their food and weather is and the Americans and the red Indians had the same so how could they not be the same" (198). In an article from 1930, Carl Jung made a similar observation: "And have you ever compared the skyline of New York or any other great American city with that of a pueblo like Taos? Have you noticed how the houses pile up in towers toward the center? Without conscious imitation America instinctively molds herself to the spectral outline of the Red Man's temperament" (Jung 199). Stein literally and figuratively puts the center (Yale students) in a direct and equal relationship to the margin (Native Americans) and asserts the creole dimension of American culture. *Everybody's Autobiography* really is about everybody, and by including and aligning herself with the Other Americans, she reminds her readers that the American genius is not at Yale but rather emerges in the exchange between the center and the margin.

Richard Wright's position as an outsider is evident throughout *Black Power,* and it echoes the marginality he experienced in the United States. Apart from men like Busia and Danquah, who exemplify the difference between Wright and the educated elite of the Gold Coast, the man he most ardently supports, Kwame Nkrumah, is deliberately inaccessible. Wright rarely saw Nkrumah, nor was he ever afforded an insider's view of the party's activities. Wright's friendship with George Padmore had secured him a visa, but it did nothing to facilitate a rapport with Nkrumah. Indeed Padmore, who had long championed Nkrumah and his cause, was treated very badly by Nkrumah's administration. Nkrumah had invited him to be part of his new government, but when Padmore arrived to assume his duties he found himself in an extremely uncooperative, almost hostile, environment. The situation never improved (Hooker 132–39). At one political rally, Wright noticed that the participants took an oath to Nkrumah. Initially stunned, he later decided that this was a fusion of tribalism and modern politics. Twice Wright asked Nkrumah for a copy of the oath, and the Prime Minister ignored him. At another party rally, Wright made a brief but enthusiastic speech in support of Nkrumah. Afterwards a reporter asked Wright for permission to print the speech. Wright then turned to Nkrumah for directions. The prime minister requested his notes, looked them over, and then placed them in the breast pocket of Wright's suit. Wright's relations with Nkrumah and his deputies never improved; frequent visits to Nkrumah's headquarters elicited no information. The final blow came when, after Wright requested an itinerary for a trip into the jungle, Nkrumah's people referred him to the British.

South African author Peter Abrahams recalled a meeting with Wright in Accra. Wright was "surprised that even educated Africans, racially conscious literate people, had not heard of him and were skeptical of a grown man earning his living by writing" (45). Wright may not have expected to feel at home in the Gold Coast, with Nkrumah or his party members, but what made him experience his marginality in ways he may not have expected was the extent to which everyone seemed to know where and to whom he/she belonged: "If you are a tribal stranger, you seek out your tribe and you are taken care of. If you are a European, you seek the shelter of the European community. But an American Negro is an oddity; he has one foot in both worlds and he pays through the nose for what he gets" (315).

The journey throughout the Gold Coast ends as it began, with a funeral and a meditation on slavery. Before returning to Accra, Wright stopped to take photographs of another funeral procession. As he focused the camera, one of the participants warned him not to take any pictures, but another man urged him to proceed. Other men were consulted, and they agreed that he could take two photos. Again he focused the camera, but this time a man ran toward him brandishing a knife, screaming, "Take no picture. I kill you . . . You work for British" (330). Twice Wright shouted, "I'm an American!" (330). In an echo of Busia's assertion that in critical moments all people fall back on the deepest teachings of their lives, Wright's response was not to claim his race but his native land, where ironically he learned everything he would ever need to know about racism and marginality. For Stein and Wright the relationship of the perceived center to the margins, the sense of distance and alienation, was the dynamic of which modernity and modernist art was made.

Stein and Wright invite us to explore the relationship between the narratives of their journeys "home" to their earlier imaginative literature. *Everybody's Autobiography* refers to *The Autobiography of Alice B. Toklas* and is itself a refutation of autobiography as genre. *Black Power* refers explicitly to *Native Son* and implicitly to *Black Boy*. In *Everybody's Autobiography* and *Black Power,* the authors "worry" the distinction between fact and fiction, privileging a poetic truth over prosaic fact. Also at work, and perhaps more important for this discussion, is the relationship between travel (leaving home/ returning home/visiting the home of one's ancestors) knowledge and the imagination. Stephen Greenblatt makes the following observation about Herodotus, but the formulation works as well for Stein and Wright: "Knowledge depends upon the refusal to be bound within the walls of the city. Knowledge depends upon travel, upon a refusal to respect boundaries, upon a restless drive toward the margins" (*Marvelous* 127). The link between their meditations on origins, homes lost and found, and creativity suggests yet another way in which their marginality and the modernist sensibility are figured. This is especially true for Wright because, unlike Stein—who spent her earliest years shuttling between Europe and North America, between Vienna and Paris, between French, English, and German— his foreign travel took place only after he had published *Uncle Tom's Children* and *Native Son.* Wright's early career makes clear the relationship between reading, travel, and imaginative work.

Before leaving for America, Stein discussed the problem of narration with Thornton Wilder: "No one in our time had really been able to tell anything without anything but just telling that thing and I was going to try once more . . . to simply tell something" (107). In another conversation with Wilder after her journey to the States, Stein expressed the same concern: "I had not simply told anything and I wanted to do that thing . . . I would simply say what was happening which is what is narration, and I must do it" (302). Stein confesses that this has been her goal for *Everybody's Autobiography,* which she then compares to *The Autobiography of Alice B. Toklas.* In the latter she had merely described what had happened, whereas in the former she had tried to write a simple narrative, "as if it is existing simply that thing" (302). She concludes tentatively, "And now in this book I have done it if I have done it" (303). But Stein's doubts of whether she has accomplished this creep up again a few pages later: "I am writing and then I get worried lest I have succeeded and it is too commonplace and too simple so much so that it is nothing" (310). Stein worried about whether America or her own literary experiments were in fact interesting "even if there was no water in the ocean of it."

The laconic quality of American speech is one of its many features Stein admired. For linked to this quality is the sense of timing she considered to be a fundamentally American trait: "Before I left America I had visited almost thirty universities and I began to really like only that, there were lots more of them where I would have liked to have gone we only got to know about some of them after we had left where they were but it would be fun to go to every one of them all over the United States, I sometimes think it would be fun to talk to students in every university all over the world, it would be interesting and they would like it as well as I would because of course they would like it, and certainly I liked the thirty I did visit" (215). If narrative were done correctly, these mostly monosyllabic words would replicate "immediate existing," that is in Stein's idiom, to make narrative as immediate as experience.

Wright's reference to *Black Boy* is clearest in the interpolated tale and interview with the young man from Labadi. The most interesting references in *Black Power* are to *Native Son.* Wright walked out of a special session of the legislature (partly in disgust) and went to the movies. He bought a ticket for the gallery to sit near the young people he had seen on the streets. The film was an American Western, and Wright marveled at the "uproarious detachment" of the viewers; after several minutes Wright realized that no one was interested in the plot. Instead each scene had its own particular interest: when a character fell, everyone laughed; during a love scene, they "hooted"; and during a chase, they shouted, "Go, go, go, go, go . . . !" (173). Wright concluded: "Psychologically distant, they mocked at a world that was not their own, had their say about a world in which they had no say" (173).

In *Native Son,* Bigger and Jack join an audience apparently like the one just described. In the first film, a wild-looking man pursues a rich woman in an elite supper club. As the man approaches her table, the audience shouts, "Stop 'im! Grab 'im!" When the man pulls a black object from his coat, they yell, "He's got a bomb! Stop 'im." The bomb-toting young man is a communist and the jealous lover of the woman whose husband he is trying to kill (27–28). Drawing a parallel between the plot of the film and the plot of Bigger's odyssey foreshadows the chain of events, but it also underscores the distance between the reality of a young black man from the ghetto and the larger-than-life world of his white employer.

Even though the responses of the audiences are similar, their perspectives on the films they watch are qualitatively different. The African audience is not concerned with the narrative, only the separate moments of action. The African-American audience is drawn into the plot so much that they express concern when the heroine's life is endangered. In *Black Power*, Wright uses the audience's response to illustrate the young Africans' distance from the white Western world. In *Native Son*, the audience's response illustrates the more complex relationship between black and white Americans. Young, unemployed, black men from the ghetto watching a film depicting a rich white woman at a supper club emphasize the social and economic schism between these groups. At the same time, Bigger is, to some extent, a sympathetic viewer. Wright makes this point through Bigger's reaction to the second film, which takes place in Africa. As Bigger watches, the pictures of "naked black men and women whirling in wild dances" are replaced in his mind with "images . . . of white men and women dressed in black and white clothes, laughing, talking, drinking and dancing" (29). As he tries to decide between robbing Blum's store or taking the job for the Daltons, Bigger recalls a story of a black chauffeur marrying a rich white girl whose parents provide them with a lot of money before sending them out of the country. Bigger's response to Hollywood's version of Africa is to "frown." He cannot empathize with the "black men and women dancing free and wild, men and women who were adjusted to their soil and at home in their world, secure from fear and hysteria" (29). Bigger would have to find the white world more plausible because he could not imagine a world in which black men and women were "at home in their world" (29).

The second reference to *Native Son* is curious. During his trip into the interior, Wright visited a factory run by a British couple. The woman, extremely concerned that Wright give a fair portrait of their enterprise, tried to ascertain whether he was a communist. Wright found these attempts laughable and enjoyed confounding her. He answered one of her questions with a straightforward lie, and to other questions his responses are misleading; he is right at home with the African trickster. When she asked if he sat in the front seat with his driver, Wright replied, "Oh, no. I sit in the *back*, . . . He's my driver" (317). Wright then adds, "She had the queer notion that a Communist would have ridden up in the front seat with his chauffeur! And she felt that if I had been a Communist, I'd have told her that I did" (318). In this context, we might assume that Wright did not tell her the truth. It is not clear from the text where he actually sat. Given the heat and the bad roads, it is likely that he sat wherever he was most comfortable. What is curious is the comment that this woman had the "queer notion that a Communist would have ridden up front." Yet this is exactly what Jan Erlone and Mary Dalton do in *Native Son*. This gesture, like the handshake and the first-name familiarity, provokes Bigger's confusion and hostility. In the novel it adds to the grim chain of events; in *Black Power*, Wright dismisses it as a "queer notion." This woman might have just read Wright's most famous novel and, to discover whether he too was a communist, decided to use one of his own indices. Wright, wanting to make a distinction between the "facts" of *Black Power* and the fiction of *Native Son*, glossed over the idea as if it had sprung from an overly active imagination. That Wright includes this anecdote draws attention to the parallel that then functions to blur the distinction between fiction and nonfiction.

Stein and Wright play with the distinction between fact and fiction, character and author in a way that figures their meditations on identity throughout their narratives. In *Everybody's Autobiography*, Stein's American journey concludes with a visit to Oakland that prompted her second-most-quoted quip: "What was the use of my having come from Oakland it was not natural to have come from there yes write about it if I like . . . but not there, there is no there there" (289). For Stein, the confrontation with her past is unsettling because it forces her to consider the contradiction at the center of human experience: "there is no limit to space and yet one is living in a limited space and inside oneself there is no sense of time but actually one is always living in time" (243). For a writer who always wanted to be "historical," history is never quite right because it is never quite finished: "The minute you or anybody else knows what you are you are not it, you are what you or anybody else knows you are and as everything in living is made up of finding out what you are it is extraordinarily difficult really not to know what you are and yet to be that thing. Very difficult indeed because not alone you but the whole country in which you have your being has to be like that" (92). Here the impossibility of a definitive self is aligned with America, itself in process. There is, however, another dimension to the problem of identity, fact and fiction, truth and the abjectly true.

One of William James's most enduring gifts to Gertrude Stein was the Socratic freedom not to have a solution. Having met with many college students, Stein concluded that they were not so different from herself or her peers four decades earlier. The portrait of young Gertrude Stein at Radcliffe College is strangely poignant. She recalls that in the 1890s Darwin's theory of evolution was still exciting. "Science meant everything" (242). Unlike religion or philosophy, science was not merely a solution but a solution that led to another problem. Paraphrasing James, Stein wrote, "Science is not a solution and not a problem it is a statement of the observation of things observed and perhaps not interesting perhaps therefore only abjectly true" (242). Ultimately the "variability and indeterminacy of human identity" is confirmed even in, or especially with, a homecoming.

Stein links this to the problem of writing autobiography: "That is the trouble with an autobiography you do not of course you do not really believe yourself why should you, you know so well so very well that it is not yourself, it could not be yourself because you cannot remember right and if you do remember right it does not sound right and of course it does not sound right because it is not right. You are of course never yourself" (70). Ultimately Stein's "homecoming" is less those months she spent talking and listening to "everybody" than it is her account of it. And very much like the indeterminate human identity, it insists on process and on contingency. We conclude where we began with the title's nouns, which self-destruct even as we say them. Yet the effect is not to destroy the possibility of meaning but, rather, like the anecdote, to "introduce an opening" to suggest other possible meanings, to resist the definitive.

In an essay on *Black Power*, K. Anthony Appiah takes issue with Wright's treatment of the African body. He notes instances where Wright's encounter with seminude, diseased, or misshapen (by Western standards) bodies provoked revulsion. Appiah argues that this tactic was part of a mechanism by which Wright makes alien that which is familiar. Appiah confesses: "I was raised in the Ghana that Nkrumah's Gold Coast became. I spent my youth in the landscape and among the people Wright seeks to anatomize; and what strikes me repeatedly is the way that *Black Power* de familiarizes a world I know" (183). But Wright did not need to "de familiarize" a world that he did not know. Appiah criticizes Wright's repetitive use of "black" to describe the African "bodyscape." In so doing, Appiah argues Wright could underscore the central paradox of the book: "I was black and they were black, but my blackness did not help me" (127). But *Black Power* also reveals the delight of an African American in a black man's country: "I saw Africa for the first time . . . black life was everywhere . . . I was startled by a European family threading its way through the black crowd. . . . We walked past black traffic officers, black policemen, gangs of black workmen; . . . in the locomotive of a train, I saw a black fireman and a black engineer. The whole of life that met the eyes was black" (34). Wright passes villages where "naked black children sat . . . playing" and "black women, naked to the waist, were washing their multicolored cloths in shallow, muddy rivers," and is reminded of Georgia or his native Mississippi (36). Soon however a mild panic sets in and he waits for "these fantastic scenes to fade" (37). "My protest was not against Africa or its people; it was directed against the unsettled feeling engendered by the strangeness of a completely different order of life" (37).

Even as he celebrated the fact that for the first time in his life, he was in a country where black men and women were the majority, it was disorienting. Wright's repetition of the adjective "black" is an effort to absorb the shock. The word "black" initially appears before every description of every person he sees and draws attention to the novelty of the experience. But the continued repetition of the word has the opposite effect; toward the middle and by the conclusion of the text, "black" ceases to have the same impact. Repetition, as Wright learned from Gertrude Stein, eventually empties a word of its conventional meaning. This narrative strategy underscores the significant discovery suggested by the statement, "I was black and they were black, but my blackness did not help me." Beyond pointing to the central paradox of the text, this statement challenges the idea of race as a fixed and absolute component in the construction of identity.

Wright openly admits what few writers about Africa ever had. Invoking St. Paul, he writes: "Africa is a vast, dingy mirror and what modern man sees in that mirror he hates. . . . He thinks, when looking into that mirror, that he is looking at black people who are inferior, but, really, he is looking at himself and, unless he possesses a superb knowledge of himself, his first impulse is to . . . smash this horrible image of himself which his soul projects upon this Africa" (158). Wright is not the first to employ this metaphor to express seeing the "Other" through "a glass darkly," but his application of it is original. For example Werner Sollors notes Jean Toomer's *Cane* in the section entitled "Bona and Paul." This narrative "opposes imaginative vision to ethnic blindness of a priori assumptions" (*Beyond* 253). St. Paul's formula assumes progression: "For now we see through a glass, darkly; but then face to face: now I know in part; but then shall I know even as also I am known" (1 Corinthians 13:14). Wright's use of the metaphor does not assume the progress suggested by "now . . . but then." The "vast, dingy mirror" reflects the darkness of the spectator's own soul. And if a "superb" a priori self-knowledge exists, only then might he suppress the impulse to destroy what he sees. Beyond the eloquence of this passage is Wright's recognition that Africa would reveal more about the viewer than about itself. This passage recalls Joseph Conrad's *Heart of Darkness*; Wright's "vast, dingy mirror" parallels Conrad's metaphor for the "darkness" not of Africa but of Kurtz's soul. Unlike earlier "explorers" of Africa, Wright could not look upon this world with "imperial eyes." Pratt argues that from the beginning, Wright is interested in "parodying and reworking the inherited tropology" of travel literature, beginning with his refusal of the balcony and the "monarch-of-all-I-survey-scene" (221–22). Indeed, part of Wright's project has been to demonstrate the extent to which the West, even an African American, will fail to see Africa.

For both writers, it was impossible to think of human identity as something definitive. To do so would have meant a capitulation to a world and world order in which they had never had a voice, and one they believed was in the process of change. Stein began first to express it in her syntax. After World War II, poetics and politics came together in works like *Brewsie and Willie* and *The Mother of Us All.* Wright's work began with a commitment to both politics and poetics that would be grounded in the drama of black life in America. His career is a logical consequence for the creator of *Black Boy,* which invariably moved him outside the confines of the Negro writer of protest fiction to the international writer-at-large.

4 Lecture Notes:
Gertrude Stein's *Lectures in America* and Richard Wright's *White Man, Listen!*

One cannot come back too often to the question what is knowledge and to the answer knowledge is what one knows.

Gertrude Stein

In a letter dated October 29, 1945, Richard Wright urged Gertrude Stein to return to the States for a lecture tour. The moment was ideal; the postwar period had opened people's minds, and they needed new ideas: "The nation feels guilty right now about the Negro and if you came and hammered it home while they feel that way, why, they would sit back and take notice. I have in mind . . . something like this: You'd speak mainly to the artists. You'd tell them, why you dumb bunnies, French artists know more of Negro life in Africa than you do about Negro life in the United States. . . . I was the first to treat Negro life seriously in my *Three Lives*; now what in hell have you white artists . . . been doing since I showed you the way? . . . I think that would jar quite a few of them." Wright adds that encouragement from her would make young black writers more confident. The lecture's topic was not far from Stein's own concerns in postwar Europe, nor was the idea of lecturing a nation in social crisis. Stein's first lecture tour took place at the nadir of the Great Depression. *Lectures in America* (1935) and *White Man, Listen!* (1957) were delivered during critical moments in American and world history. Both collections are offered as record and expression of each writer's developing awareness of the larger transformations we ascribe to the modern and postmodern world.

Despite the differences in content, the collections are linked in several ways. Stein's lectures address the development of the radical transformation of American literature at the turn of the century. The rupture, dislocation-location, distance, and mimetic alienation we link to Stein's experimental modernism would become the grammar and syntax with which the radical, young thinker Richard Wright described and demanded new social and political forms. Through these lectures, we begin to appreciate the implications of their journeys, both actual and imaginative. The lectures address the epistemological crisis in our brave new world. The collections develop further these ideas: that cultural values are relative; that a psychological model forces us to rethink the meaning of self and society; that the essentialist categories of race, gender, and ethnicity must be reconsidered; that modern and postmodern poetics and politics are informed by a new experience of the temporal.

By 1933 when Stein wrote *Lectures in America,* she had already spent several years trying to develop a theoretical context that would clarify the confusion surrounding her work. In 1926 she delivered a lecture, "Composition As Explanation," at the Literary Society of Cambridge University and at Oxford and London Universities. Other early essays on aesthetics were "An Elucidation" in *Portraits and Prayers* and "Regular Regularly In Narrative" in *How To Write* (Bridgman 66–175). The act of public speaking gave her much anxiety; the issues of audience expectation and artistic integrity are already apparent in these early lectures. More challenging for Stein was the task of conveying her sense of the New to academic audiences, the gatekeepers of the Tradition. But the popularity of *The Autobiography* made her an intriguing figure, and the lectures were well attended all over the country.

The first lecture, "What Is English Literature," begins: "One cannot come back too often to the question what is knowledge and to the answer knowledge is what one knows" (11). Stein qualifies this apparent tautology by adding, "those of us that have always had the habit of reading have our own history of English literature inside us, the history as . . . we have come to know it" (13). The emphasis is wholly subjective, and yet this is Stein's primary focus. The questions, as Wendy Steiner notes, are not raised to be answered but rather "to decide about knowing" (Introduction xxiv). To make this point, Stein takes us through her own thought process:

What does literature do and how does it do it. And what does English literature do and how does it do it. And what ways does it use to do what it does do. If it describes what it sees how does it do it. If it describes what it knows how does it do it and what is the difference between what it sees and what it knows. And then too there is what it feels and then also there is what it hopes and wishes . . . and then there is what it explains. To do any or all of these things different things have been done. Most of them are being done all the time by literature. And how has English literature done it. (14)

For Stein, geography and history produce a nation's aesthetic, "The glory of English literature is description simple concentrated description of . . . what exists and so what makes the life the island life the daily island life" (14–15). England is Eden, where in the beginning, there was no discrepancy between the sign and the signified. But dramatic historical events provoked drastic changes in literary expression. In the nineteenth century, at the height of English imperialism, writers wrote more self-consciously. Owning not only their island but everything outside of it compels them to explain: "You naturally begin to explain that to yourself and you also begin to explain it to those living your daily life who own it with you, everything outside, and you naturally explain it in a kind of way to some of those whom you own" (41). But what if those you "own" see it, experience it otherwise? What if colonized Caliban (here Stein means Americans) learns the King's English to better curse him? Stein will leave the political dimension of her observation for the next generation.

Even though nineteenth-century American literature shared qualities with British literature, it expressed a very different sensibility because "it was not leading a daily island life . . . That is fundamental that is what the American writing inevitably is, it is not a daily life at all" (46). Henry James's work is the best example of the key difference between an English and an American aesthetic: "the disembodied way of disconnecting something from anything" (53). James's writing possessed a "future feeling" unlike the English, where the paragraph, in this example, expressed the sense of "ending" (52). Stein adds: "I went on to what was the American thing the disconnection and I kept breaking the paragraph down . . . to commence again with not connecting with the daily anything and yet to really choose something" (54). The quality of movement is what differentiates American life and literature from that of the English. Americans are on the move even when they stand still, whereas the English, "even when they are traveling are not moving" (*Narration* 11). This movement is represented in American literature by a detachment of words from "the solidity of anything, they began to excitedly feel themselves as if they were anywhere or anything" (*Narration* 10). Americans had inherited a language that could not, given the facts of geography and history, express its own sensibility.

Stein's assessment of the American literary tradition fits into Werner Sollors's paradigm of American identity as both inherited and chosen. Americans inherited the English language and then chose new modes of expression that made it particular to their experience. Stein cites Whitman as the premier example of this; the difference in American and British poetics is most vivid when Whitman's *Leaves of Grass* is compared to Tennyson's *Idylls of the King*. Stein describes how Americans took English words and by rearranging them, putting pressure on them, achieved new expression: "And they [Americans] did this thing and they are doing this thing and punctuation and arranging them and destroying any connection between them between the words that would that did when the English used them make of them having a beginning and a middle and an ending . . . made of these English words words that move as the Americans move with them move always move in every direction and in any direction" (*Narration* 14). The conventional literary forms had to be remade to express an American sensibility just as American identity had to reflect the combination of an inherited and a chosen identity. Stein's innovations are the earliest expression of American modernism. And paradoxically, Stein's sense of herself as Other helped her to articulate the difference between American and British literature, in part because "ethnic writers, alerted to cultural clashes, may feel the need for new forms earlier or more intensely than mainstream authors" (Sollors 247). Stein transforms inherited English literary forms into a viable mode of expression for American writers. She concludes, "Really there is no choice. Nobody chooses" (54). Writers who are keenly aware of their time and place write in the manner that best fits the particulars of their personal experience and that is rooted in the land by which they were formed: "I like the feeling of words doing as they want to do and as they have to do when they live where they live" (*Narration* 15). Addressing the political dimension of the revolution in worldview that Stein's poetics express, Wright's focus is postcolonial Africa.

Between 1950 and 1956, Richard Wright wrote and delivered three of the four lectures that comprise *White Man, Listen!* These lectures address the problems of the newly emerging nations in the postcolonial period. Wright's European audiences were slowly recovering from World War II. The French and English bitterly fought the end of colonialism in Africa and Asia, and the European continent had become the battlefield of the Cold War. Wright's role in these lectures, as in the one lecture written before his expatriation, is that of the articulate Marginal Man who announces and elucidates the new era in human history.

Wright devoted most of his time and energy between 1952 and 1958 to understanding the origins of modernity through colonialization and American slavery. In addition to the travel works *Black Power* and *Pagan Spain,* he published an account of the Bandung Conference, *The Color Curtain: A Report of the Bandung Conference,* in 1956. Wright contributed to the founding of the journal *Présence Africaine* and was among the principal organizers of the First Congress of Negro Artists and Writers, which took place in September 1956. One of Wright's challenges as mediator was to demonstrate to American and European audiences the ways in which these emerging nations adapted and transformed Western political forms.

Wright's goal was to win sympathy for these nationalist movements from Western governments, particularly the United States.

"The Miracle of Nationalism in the African Gold Coast" begins with a dramatic format: "TIME: *The middle of the twentieth century.* PLACE: *The hot and lush high rain forest of British West Africa*" (151). Wright then lists the dramatis personae, most of whom are African, but also included are British merchants, officials, missionaries, and intelligence agents. Wright addresses the audience directly, and although this narrative takes place in the West African jungle, every member of the European audience has played a role. The presentation of Kwame Nkrumah's fight for Ghanaian independence in a dramatic format makes Wright's larger point; it describes the most dramatic event of the twentieth century because it marks a break in the five-hundred-year history of European dominance of Africa.

The drama culminates in a secret late-night meeting in 1948 among six Africans who formed a group called the Secret Circle and devoted themselves to Ghanaian independence. Mirroring the portrait of this elite he had drawn in *Black Power,* Wright argues that these men felt alienated from the West, where they had been educated, and from their native Africa. They were also united in their antipathy for the "black bourgeoisie," whom they regarded as British "stooges." They had to decide on a plan to obtain political independence from the British without conceding power to the bourgeoisie. Their greatest challenge would be to galvanize an illiterate population to act under their direction. This African elite would be familiar to American audiences because these men have the African-American's "double consciousness."

Wright's freedom fighters also sound like secular humanists and die-hard democrats. One member argues that to forge solidarity behind their movement, the Secret Circle must appeal to the people's pride in their cultural and religious traditions. But he quickly adds, "Now, gentlemen, I realize that we do not believe in such mumbo jumbo, and all the childish rituals that such traditions imply. But we have no other basis upon which to make a call for unity" (157). The men decide to resume traditional tribal dress; "in order to go forward, we must go backward a step or two" (157). Suddenly the story takes an odd twist: the members of the Secret Circle seal this pact by swearing fetish. Why would Westernized Africans swear fetish? "I have contended that these men were Westernized. They were. But they lived amidst tribal conditions of life and they reacted to ancestor-worshipping values. . . . Thus their world was compounded half of Europe and half of Africa. . . . They lived in two worlds. BUT THEY DIDN'T REALLY BELIEVE IN EITHER OF THOSE WORLDS. THE WORLD THAT THEY REALLY WANTED, THE WORLD THAT WOULD BE THE HOME OF THEIR HEARTS, HAD NOT YET COME INTO BEING" (170; Wright's emphasis). Wright argues that all men are in part rational and in part irrational, adding that "what makes other men seem outlandish to us is our lack of imagination" (171).

Wright resists the idea that this elite is bound to their traditional beliefs, as indeed Danquah and Busia argue it was, but he accords those beliefs an important role in the struggle for independence. This registers a shift in his initial position: "The unspoken assumption in this history has been: WHAT IS GOOD FOR EUROPE IS GOOD FOR ALL MANKIND! I say so be it" (98). Yet when Wright describes the many facets of Nkrumah's nationalist movement, he makes this change: "In most discussions of movements of this sort, you'll hear descriptions of constitutions, of the principles of democracy . . . you'll hear Westerners, who feel that only their assumptions are valid for all people, at all times, and everywhere, tell you how the lower orders of mankind are gradually beginning to resemble them. In contrast . . . I emphasize the primal impulses that give birth to such movements" (171).

Before visiting the Gold Coast in 1953, Wright had assumed that Nkrumah's movement would resemble that of any Western nation. But the reality of it challenged his every assumption; Wright had to reconcile the African features of a democratic independence movement with an explicitly Western goal. Such a reconciliation was possible when those features were placed in the service of that goal. The "primal impulses" are everyone's desire for political and economic independence, and few African communities needed to be persuaded of this. Wright argues that the "Africanness" of Nkrumah's movement, although culturally specific, does not detract from a fundamental and universal desire for economic and political freedom. In this way, Wright places Nkrumah's movement on a global and historical continuum. Indeed, the ability to adapt the ideal to the specific demands of time and place is the guiding principle of Stein's poetics.

Stein's account of her education in aesthetics emphasizes experience as opposed to formal training. This narrative begins in California with Stein's first memory of an oil painting, a panorama of the Battle of Waterloo. The eight-year-old was struck by the fact that, although the painting depicted the features of an outdoor setting, it was not outdoors. "I remember . . . almost consciously knowing that there was no air . . . there was no feeling of air, it was just an oil painting and it had a life of its own" (63). She compares this discovery to her first visit to Gettysburg. On a beautiful day in early summer, she recalls having enjoyed the visit and something of what she saw, "but I do not know exactly what it looked like as I know exactly what the battle of Waterloo looked like at the Panorama of the battle of Waterloo" (64). The Gettysburg memory includes a number of sensory impressions; the oil painting memory is only visual and therefore easier to recall. Through this comparison, Stein identifies an important paradox: what made the painting remarkable was not its verisimilitude but its inability to reproduce experiential reality. As such, it asserts and insists on its identity as an oil painting and nothing more. Through this anecdote, Stein makes one of the fundamental points of her decisions about oil painting, "I began to feel that it made no difference what an oil painting painted it always did and should look like an oil painting" (72). Stein's earliest aesthetic discoveries depend on perceptual distinctions.

Stein identifies verisimilitude as the most problematic aspect of painting: "you do understand that what really annoys people that is anybody who is at all annoyed by an oil painting is not its being an oil painting, but the subject" (88). Stein confesses that to some extent she is still bothered by this but then states that after having spent many years becoming "familiar" with oil paintings, she decided that the relationship between the painting and its subject was "nobody's business" (79). This realization made it possible for her to accept the radical work of first Cézanne and later Matisse and Picasso. More important, it freed her to do her own work, which incorporated the mimetic alienation of these artists. In Cézanne's work the real-life subject and artistic object were expressed simultaneously. The criterion was not based on a visual resemblance but on "vitality" or the essence of the subject. Whether he painted apples, chairs, or people, Stein argues "they were so entirely these things that they were not an oil painting and yet that is just what the Cézannes were" (77). She adds, "this was a great relief to me and I began my writing" (77). The subject of the oil painting, like the subject of a work of literature, provided the raw material, but the relationship between that raw material and the art work was not important.

Again, in "Plays," Stein establishes her authority on the genre by recalling her earliest experiences of theater. Stein confesses that the typical dramatic experience made her nervous. This nervousness is provoked by "syncopated time," which she argues results from the discrepancy between the action depicted on the stage and the apprehension of that action psychologically and emotionally by the viewer. This assessment illuminates the psychological underpinnings of her work and more.

Stein's analysis of drama begins by asking the audience to examine how they experience a play. The focus remains on the viewer's perception; the methodology is reminiscent of her training under William James: "Is the thing seen or the thing heard the thing that makes most of its impression on you at the theater. How much has hearing to do with it and how little. Does the thing heard replace the thing seen. Does it help or does it interfere with it. . . . Does the thing or does the thing heard effect you and effect you at the same time or in the same degree or does it not" (101). As a young woman, Stein confessed that she "stumbled" on these questions whenever she went to the theater. Costumes distracted her, and the actors' voices and gestures interfered with her experience of the play.

Stein's dislike for the dramatic experience was rooted in a need to control her own psychological responses. She compares theatrical "excitement" to the excitement one experiences in life or in reading literature. But in life one is an active participant with some influence or control, and in reading one can put the book down if the excitement becomes too great. Even though Stein's nervousness in the theater stemmed from a lack of control, her assessment of dramatic experience touches on one of the central concerns of modernist expression: the problem of temporal representation. Aristotle's definition of tragedy in the *Poetics* illuminates this problem.

Throughout the discussion of tragedy, Stein is diametrically opposed to Aristotle; indeed it is as if she had read him to know exactly what not to do. Aristotle argues that tragedy provides an opportunity for the audience to experience (from the safe remove of aesthetic distance) both emotional involvement and detachment. Indeed catharsis was only possible under these circumstances (Butcher x–xi). Stein calls catharsis "relief," and she does not find it a satisfying experience. Rather, catharsis is inferior to the experience of "completion" that one experiences as a participant in an exciting situation or if there is a unity of emotion and action (99–100). She concludes that the problem of temporal representation has prompted her to think about the dramatic experience in terms of emotion and time as opposed to story and action (again in opposition to Aristotle). Stein's fundamental disagreement with Aristotle is located in his first stipulation of the definition of tragedy:

> Now, according to our definition, Tragedy is an imitation of an action that is complete, and whole, and of a certain magnitude; for there may be a whole that is wanting in magnitude. A whole is that which has a beginning, a middle and an end. A beginning is that which does not itself follow anything by causal necessity, but after which something naturally is or comes to be. An end, on the contrary, is that which itself naturally follows some other thing, either by necessity, or as a rule, but has nothing following it. A middle is that which follows something as some other thing follows it. (*Poetics* 6:2–3)

Stein took every opportunity to refute this definition. In another lecture at the University of Chicago, she recapitulated this position, "I found myself . . . quite naturally using the present participle . . . I could not free myself from the present participle because I felt dimly that I had to know what I knew and I knew that the beginning and middle and ending was not where I began" (*Narration* 24). Stein's rejection of causality is one way of grappling with temporal representation; more important, it illuminates the role of the subjective in the making of modernist aesthetic. Similarly, Wright draws on (even as he criticizes) a psychological study of colonialism to illuminate the role of the subjective in social and political forms.

Wright's lecture, "The Psychological Reaction of Oppressed People," was informed by and is a response to Octave Mannoni's *Psychologie de la Colonisation.* This study was translated into English in 1956 as *Prospero and Caliban,* and Wright reviewed it for the *Nation.* Mannoni's study was based on his experience as a psychiatrist in the then French colony of Madagascar; more important, it was prompted by a 1947 Malagasy uprising in which thousands of French and Malagasy were killed. Mannoni accounts for the rebellion with a psychoanalytical model where colonized and colonizer are locked in a symbiotic relationship of mutual dependence. According to this model, the Malagasy revolted because they feared the French would abandon them before they were able to govern themselves (76–77). For Mannoni, the Malagasy who led the revolt, the Western-educated elite, were insufficiently assimilated. Frantz Fanon counters that the Malagasy rebelled when they realized that Western values, such as a respect for civil rights and political sovereignty, did not apply to them (100). For Mannoni, the source of colonial ills is located in the human psyche; for Fanon, these same maladies are the consequence of the colonial situation itself. Wright agreed that Mannoni's analysis revealed the ways in which colonialism corrupts both the oppressor and the oppressed, but, like Fanon, he objected to Mannoni's conclusions. Mannoni's treatment of the natives of Madagascar "creates the impression . . . that those natives are somehow the white man's burden" (Wright, "Neuroses" 331). Wright concludes: "Well, maybe now the other side of the coin will someday be described by black, brown and yellow men who are psychologically free enough to explain how the emotionally disturbing white faces roused them and sent them hurtling toward emotional horizons as yet distant and dim (331). The postcolonial period provoked new social, economic, and political forms. Fanon and Wright were committed to understanding colonialism through a comprehensive paradigm that included its psychological dimension. This is the thrust of *Black Skin, White Masks* and of "The Psychological Reactions of Oppressed People."

The lecture begins by describing the devastating effects of colonialism and imperialism on traditional cultures worldwide: "the ultimate effect of white Europe upon Asia and Africa was to cast millions into a kind of spiritual void" (34). "Europe blundered into the house of mankind, nullifying ancient traditions that sustained and informed the lives of millions with meaning" (42). The focus is the psychological implications of colonialism for the "tragic elite" to whom the text is dedicated. Wright argues that the complaint of the "tragic elites" with the West is in effect the West's argument with itself; it is a house divided. Wright's European audiences would come away with insight into the former colonial's point of view. As he systematically defines and redefines terms that are flash points in every colonial setting, the audiences are held responsible for colonialism's grim and ugly features.

Wright borrowed an analogy from Friederich Nietzsche to illustrate the psychological position of the educated African or Asian vis-à-vis his white counterpart, the frog perspective: "It involves a situation in which, for moral or social reasons, a person or group feels that there is another person or group above it" (27). For example, when a black American is asked to describe his situation, he will reply, "we are rising" (28). The standard against which this rise is measured is that of his "hostile white neighbor." This frog perspective characterized both the educated Asian and African elite as well as the American black. And at the Bandung Conference, Wright observed: "The core of reality today for hundreds of millions resides in how unlike the West they are and how much and quickly they must resemble the West" (29). Wright makes clear, however, the point that resembling the West is not slavish imitation; the emerging nation's challenge was to keep the West out. Using the idea of "antagonist acculturation" George Devereux and Edwin Loeb have argued that a society often adopts its adversary's means better to resist adopting its goals. Wright made the same observation: "Industrialization soon became the new religion, not because industrialization itself was . . . revered as a means of production, but because it was the only way to hoist the white man off his [the African's] back" (50).

From Caliban's point of view, Wright unpacks terms that have marked the relationship between Europeans and their former colonials: "whiteness," "white man," "savage," and *"evolueé."* For the indigenous peoples these nouns maintain the physical and psychological distance intrinsic to the "frog perspective." For much of the so-called Third World, "whiteness" constitutes an organic whole. A Frenchman might condemn the lynching of an American black and the Americans were key to the liberation of Indonesia, but for Africans and Asians the white world was one world. Anticipating the resistance this assertion would meet with in Swedish, Danish, Dutch, German, and Italian audiences, Wright urges them to recall, "Whose hands ran the business enterprises? White hands. Whose hands meted out the law? White hands. Whose hands erected churches? White hands" (31). But to complicate this gloss Wright also includes contradictory evidence. For example, an African of the Gold Coast confessed to Wright that after independence, his country would erect a statue to the English women whose friendships had encouraged and sustained them: "If it had not been for them, we would have lost" (46). This echoes Wright's experience with the American Communist Party: "Many a *black boy* in America has seized upon the rungs of the Red ladder to climb out of his Black Belt" (45; my emphasis).

In the definition of "white man" Wright claims that, although the term evokes a distinct image in the Asian and African minds, it has nothing to do with biology. "Scientifically speaking the leaders of Asia and Africa know that there is no such thing as race" (38). The term must be understood in a sociological or historical context for what it is, a component in the construction of racist ideology. For the elite Asians and Africans, the "white man" is a man with blue eyes, blond hair, and pale skin who insists that his "blood" remain pure. This phenotypical definition, following the dismissal of "race" as a viable category, is ironic. And when Wright concludes that Africans and Asians will no longer permit the white world to extract precious raw materials from their countries simply because their eyes are blue, the irony becomes a stab at the biological superiority rationale for European imperialism.

At the same time, Wright notes that an Egyptian's marriage to a European woman would be seen as a token of disloyalty by other Egyptians. "Whiteness" is the coin of the former empire that purchases betrayal. To further complicate matters Wright claims that "any African, Asian, or American Negro who would . . . deny or negate the 'whiteness' of white Europe would be branded by his colored brothers as being 'white struck,' as being 'too Western' " (39). And as he has questioned African religious traditions, he has been accused of "mulatto thinking" (39). "Whiteness" as the demon of colonial history had to be separated from what was valuable in Western thought and culture. This was a delicate issue for Wright because, although he was committed to African and Asian political and economic independence, he objected to nondemocratic, nonsecular governments. To reject Western social, political, or philosophic traditions because Europeans are white, paralleled the rejection of a people because they were black. When he was criticized for being "white struck" or "too Western," Wright encountered a familiar response; Africans as well as African Americans were as capable of the categorical rejection characteristic of racism as their white counterparts.

To address the notion of the African or Asian as "savage," Wright draws on the work of an African scholar whom he does not name and on Mannoni's study. According to the African expert, the term "savage" was more accurately a construct of the European's imagination than an accurate description of indigenous peoples. The African argues that when a tribe's social context is profoundly disrupted, members of that tribe, now without ways to make sense of reality, may well behave erratically. This, the African argues, is what usually constitutes "savage" in the minds of Westerners who, by their presence, instigated the social instability that gave rise to the behavior (33–34). Wright's use of the African source is an excellent example of presenting "the other side of the coin by black, brown or yellow writers." And since it is a view informed by Western sociology, it is also a fine example of antagonistic acculturation; the African scholar adapts Western means, a sociological analysis, to resist its goals, the definition of Africans as "savages."

Wright agrees with Mannoni that the idea of a savage is the white man's projection onto the "other" of his own repressed desires, fears, and self-hatred: "the whites had projected out upon the blacks their own guilt, fears and sexual preoccupations" (68). More important than this insight, Mannoni's psychoanalytical paradigm enables Wright to vitiate once and for all the idea of savage as an inevitable stage in mankind's evolution from lung-fish to European or white American. Offering evidence from both French and African authorities to correct the notion of "savage" renders its conventional use meaningless.

Wright attacks the French term, *evolueé*, which in the French colonies was more loathsome than "savage." This seventeenth-century fiction, still current well into the twentieth century, argued that the European presence in Africa and Asia would effect a gradual transition from the state of "savagery" to that of "civilization" in the indigenous peoples. In the aftermath of one of the most barbaric wars in human history, Wright asked who was to decide when these colonies were "civilized" enough to run their own affairs. Who indeed is civilized? Clearly the continued presence of the British and French in Africa and Asia was not furthering the cause of civilization.

In two subsections, "Men without Language" and "The Zone of Silence," Wright describes the psychological impact of colonialization on the ability to articulate that experience. Although this elite cadre is completely literate and always bilingual, the context for genuine expression has been curtailed by the colonial power. An African child in an English school learns the colonizer's version of his nation's past. There is a "hole" in the African's history because he has yet to write his own account; an important part of the freedom these men and women sought was to write their own history. Clearly Wright recalled the extent to which the history of African Americans in slavery was omitted or distorted by illustrious American historians. The intellectual elite needed a language and a historical context to tell their histories as much as they needed methods to modernize their nations. And on this point Wright's position was complex.

At the end of *Black Power*, Wright warns Nkrumah that the people of the Gold Coast "must be made to walk, forced draft, into the twentieth century!" (345). Wright does not specify a plan whereby the Gold Coast would be modernized within one generation. But because he used the word "militarize" to describe the strict and regimented structure through which this transformation would occur, he was accused of proposing a fascist state (Appiah 189–90). By "militarize" he may have been referring to martial discipline, which characterized the early days of schools like the Hampton Institute. Recall that the Hampton Institute was directed by General Samuel Armstrong, who had served with the Union forces during the Civil War. Armstrong believed that the former slaves needed the regimented structure of military life to make the daunting transition from slaves to free men. Armstrong's most illustrious student, Booker T. Washington, details the militaristic cast of the Hampton Institute's organization in *Up from Slavery*. Wright would easily have seen in the position of the newly freed slaves a parallel to the position of the newly freed colonies. Indeed a number of Africans he meets in the Gold Coast ask questions that suggest they share this same assumption. As important to a fuller gloss on this controversial sentence is its emphasis on the temporal displacement; premodern society must become modern, and fast, if democratic governments are to survive. Militaristic enterprises were intrinsic to the making of the modern world; "avant-garde" was initially a uniquely military term.

Wright, however, remained ambivalent on the best way to modernize Africa, as is demonstrated in a passage from *The Color Curtain: A Report on the Bandung Conference*. For this text, Wright had collected a number of responses to a questionnaire he had drawn up with the help of psychologist Otto Klineberg. One Dutch colonial argued that Indonesia needed a dictator because its people where not yet capable of a democracy. Wright observes: "By prescribing dictatorial methods for Indonesian needs, he was endorsing drastic measures that he never would have sanctioned for any Western nation" (31–32). But when Wright returned to this topic in the lecture, he reiterated the position outlined in *Black Power*. The elite of Africa and Asia was fearful of the West's return to dominate the economic and political life of its countries. "So, instead of democracy obtaining in the newly freed areas, something hinting of dictatorship will no doubt prevail for a while—will prevail at least until fear of the West has died down" (59). Wright supports this position with a statement from Gunnar Myrdal, then secretary of the Economic Commission for the United Nations: "If, as is assumed to be urgent necessity in the underdeveloped countries, the movement toward industrialization is to be pushed ahead, the *state* will have to intervene" (59). Wright agreed particularly because this policy promised to keep the West out, but he also saw the problem of modernization as more fundamental than mere economic development.

As Wright saw it, the task of the new leadership was to transform tribal peoples into nations organized on principles that had developed in the wake of the Protestant Reformation: "This elite learned how Europe . . . had rolled back the tide of religion and had established the foundations of the modern state, secular institutions, free speech, science" (60). Indeed Wright saw the problem as having to transform in one or two generations premodern, God-centered societies with modern or postmodern, secular, mankind-centered communities. Wright's analysis raises the problem of temporal distance between premodern and modern or postmodern societies, for the ways in which a society experiences time determines its sense of reality. To illustrate this very problem for her generation, Gertrude Stein turned to the fundamental components of literature.

In the lecture "Poetry and Grammar," Gertrude Stein returns to challenge literary conventions with an attack on punctuation and grammar. Despite the inclination to smile at her humorous points, punctuation and parts of speech do, as any reader of Toomer or Faulkner knows, influence the way we read and comprehend narrative. Stein examines every component of the sentence, piece by piece; she dismisses the question mark, the exclamation point, and quotation marks, noting that "anybody who can read at all knows when a question is a question as it is written in writing" (215). She then examines the impact of periods, commas, colons, semicolons, and capitalization on writing. "I have had a long and complicated life with all these" (216). Early in her career she admits having been "completely possessed by the necessity that writing should go on" (217). As such, she simply could not employ the colon, semicolon, or the comma. "A comma by helping you along holding your coat for you and putting on your shoes keeps you from living your life as actively as you should" (220). The comma interferes with the sentence's vitality. "A long complicated sentence should force itself upon you, make you know yourself knowing it and the comma . . . lets you stop and take a breath" (221).

Every age and every language decides what merits capitalization. And to underscore the larger point, that such practices are conventional, Stein, adopting a French practice, never capitalizes "french" or "english." Similarly the French do not capitalize the days of the week, and since these practices are quite arbitrary, she concludes that one could do as one pleased. For unlike the marks of punctuation, capitalization had "nothing to do with the inner life of sentences or paragraphs" (222). Language, from the phoneme to the epic must express the ethos of its time and its place, and this imperative animates her discussion of the parts of speech.

Stein evaluates the parts of speech based on how effectively each conveys her perception of the modern period; indeterminacy, distance, vitality, and the unfinished are her guiding principles. Verbs and adverbs are good because they are "on the move," and the indeterminacy of prepositions makes them the perfect vehicle for the modern ethos. "Prepositions can live one long life being really nothing but absolutely nothing but mistaken" (212). Articles are varied, delicate and alive, but the noun is "so unfortunately so completely unfortunately the name of something" (212). Pronouns are acceptable because "they represent some one but they are not its or his name . . . they already have a greater possibility of being something than if they were as a noun is the name of anything" (213–14). Proper nouns are not as objectionable as common nouns because they too might vary; the chief failing of the noun is its stultifying rigidity. Slang develops out of the impulse to change nouns, "which have been names for so long" (214). In the United States slang becomes a part of conventional language more quickly than it does in more tradition-bound France. The qualities Stein admired in literature emerge in this assessment of the parts of speech. Writing must be "on the move"; it must be varied and imprecise and must reflect the indeterminacy of the modern era.

But it was the much-abused noun that best expressed poetry: "Poetry is concerned with using with abusing, with losing with wanting, with denying with avoiding with adoring with replacing the noun. Poetry is doing nothing more but using losing refusing and pleasing and betraying and caressing nouns" (231). In this definition of poetry Stein insists on verbs to challenge the fixity of a noun. She discusses this observation in "What Is English Literature." In her platonic characterization, nouns could initially express the things to which they referred, now however they inadequately name the passion one feels toward its referent. A superior poet like Whitman attempted to "express the thing and not call it by its name" (241). Or to create, as Shakespeare had, the forest of Arden "without mentioning the things that make a forest. You feel it all but he does not name its names" (236). Whitman attacked the problem formally, and Stein's own efforts to "break the rigid form of the noun" continues in this tradition. In the famous "Rose is a rose is a rose," Stein argues that she "caressed completely caressed and addressed a noun" (231). The form forces the reader to apprehend the noun "rose" in an entirely new way. For language to remain vital, it must challenge habitual modes of human expression. "Poetry and Grammar" further illustrates the extent to which literary conventions, like the cultures that produce them, are not absolute and fixed but contingent and fluid. Wright explores this thesis in his discussion of African-American literature.

"The Literature of the Negro in the United States" was written as early as 1945 for white American audiences. One of the early versions of "The Literature of the Negro in the United States" indicates that Wright may have written the lecture in late 1945 or early 1946. Nina Cobb reports that a copy of a similar speech is in the Webb Collection at the Schomburg Library. It is entitled "Speech for a

White Audience" and was written shortly after World War II (239, n.18). A French translation, "Littérature noire américaine," appeared in *Les Temps Modernes* in 1948. In this lecture, Wright's explicit objective is to demonstrate that race, in its biological sense, is unrelated to a people's aesthetic choices. Rather, through a consideration of African-American literary history, Wright argues that historical and social contexts decide how writing is written. The Middle Passage, the European conquest of the Americas, and the transformation of large populations from traditional to modern are at the center of African-American literary history.

Wright begins with an analogy; compare the provincial life of Quebec with that of any modern American city. One is a cohesive traditional whole and the other an aggregate of disparate pieces. The journey from village to city parallels the transition from Old World to New and from traditional to modern society. Modernity might result in a secular world where an individual might find his/her noblest expression, but it would also produce a society of anxious, deracinated people where crime, corruption, and racism rule. Every white American had an ancestor who had made the transition from traditional to modern, had come from some European village to begin a new life in the American maelstrom. But African Americans were forcibly taken from their homelands and sold into abject slavery where for centuries they lived "in an atmosphere of rejection and hate" (108). Despite this difference in their histories, both black and white Americans had had to make the transition from traditional to modern, and this makes their histories shared and comparable: "It is the same life lifted to the heights of pain and pathos, drama and tragedy. The history of the Negro in America is the history of America written in vivid and bloody terms; it is the history of Western Man writ small. It is the history of men who tried to adjust themselves to a world whose laws, customs, and instruments of force were leveled against them. The Negro is America's metaphor" (108–9). In this context Wright surveys the history of African-American poetry.

When a poet is at home in his/her society, skin color is the least important feature of his/her identity, and to illustrate this point Wright includes an excerpt from *The Count of Monte Cristo* by

Alexander Dumas and a piece by Alexander Pushkin. He prods, "Did a Negro write that? It does not sound Negroid" (111). Similarly, and even though she was a slave, Phillis Wheatley, like Dumas and Pushkin, identified herself as a Christian and a colonist committed to the aspirations of the fledgling nation. Wright points to "His Excellency General Washington" to illustrate Wheatley's allegiance to America's struggle for independence. In contrast, the poetry of George Moses Horton and James Whitfield express "the fact of separation from the culture of his native land. . . . The Negro loves his land, but that land rejects him" (119). After Emancipation, African-American poetry expresses the frustration and complexity of Reconstruction and Jim Crow America.

The black community becomes divided between the relatively rich and educated and the illiterate poor, a division that contributes to the kinds of poetry to emerge. Educated black Americans believed that they would be accepted by the white majority; consequently they wrote within the literary tradition. But the poor, resigned to their fate, took comfort in religion, alcohol, and the "sensualization of their suffering in the form of jazz and blues and folk and work songs" (123). This spectrum is illustrated by Du Bois's *The Souls of Black Folk* on one end and blues, work songs, and the bawdy verses called "The Dirty Dozens" on the other. Class differences aside, even the most privileged black Americans were ultimately dependent not on American justice but on philanthropy. When, after World War I, many black American veterans returned home to be lynched in uniform, the new mood among this group became outrage. In his study of lynching Walter White wrote, "It is commonly observed that after the First World War many lynchings of Negro soldiers—sometimes in uniform—were openly motivated by the fear that they had gotten 'wrong ideas' about their social status while serving in France" (111). During such periods of crisis, other components of identity, class, gender, and education were subsumed by white America's brutal imposition of race as the only meaningful component of one's identity.

So it is possible to compare James Weldon Johnson's "Brothers" (Johnson was, according to Wright, "as conservative a Negro as ever lived in America" [135]) to Wright's own poem "Between the World and Me" because lynching is the poems' shared theme. Wright's distinction illustrates George Devereux's point: "a hypercathecting of one's ethnic identity leads . . . to a drastic reduction of one's relevant class [i.e., classification] identities and thus to the annihilation of the individual's real identity. The same occurs when only one of a person's class identities is deemed relevant" (66). The mood shifted again when Marxism offered black Americans an alternative interpretation of their past and present: "Then, for the first time since Phillis Wheatley, the Negro began to make a wholehearted commitment to a new world" (142).

Wright's lecture does not consider the aesthetic and formal elements of African-American poetry because this might have detracted from his central concern, which is to illuminate specific historical and social circumstances of African-American poetry. In the 1937 essay "Blueprint for Negro Writing," Wright argues that themes for black American writers "will emerge when they have begun to feel the meaning of the history of their race as though they in one lifetime had lived it themselves throughout all the long centuries" (47). This includes knowledge and understanding of that history, not simply the facts of the Middle Passage, or of slavery, but what they mean for the present. And to arrive at an understanding of this history Wright insists that the writer see this history in its global context, to show in one's writing the relationship between the black woman hoeing cotton in Dixie and the men on Wall Street (46). To do this effectively the black writer had to be free to draw on the entire spectrum of literary ancestors: "Eliot, Stein, Joyce, Proust, Hemingway and Anderson, Gorky, Barbusse, Nexo and Jack London no less the folklore of the Negro himself should form the heritage of the Negro writer. Every iota of gain in human thought and sensibility should be ready grist for his mill, no matter how far fetched they may seem in their immediate implications" (45). Quite explicitly here Wright urges and encourages the black writer to find in folklore and modernist writing new ways with which to think and write; the African-American experience demanded nothing less.

Nearly twenty years later, Wright expanded this point in notes for a lecture in Bandung: "The increasing modernization of life made it impossible for any sensitive artist to accept the old forms of expression. Walt Whitman broke the old molds . . . The reason was not . . . willfulness, it was necessity. But new forms quickly became accepted; and this made Gertrude Stein say that classics were what had been classified. I'm . . . for the new free forms, forms conforming to the new experience, but I feel that such forms ought to be justified by their burden of organically felt passion rather than sheer technical ability" (Fabre, *Richard Wright* 152). Modernity is the catalyst for the emergence of new forms, and this model resists the essentialism of a racial ideology.

In "The Gradual Making of the Making of Americans" and in "Tradition and Industrialization," Stein and Wright turn respectively to the remarkable feature of modernity: the experience of time. Stein's lecture recalls her struggle to represent the temporal as a newly focused psychological lens demanded, and Wright grapples with the temporal displacement of African and Asian societies that must leap from premodern to modern in a single bound. The problem of the temporal animates the search for new forms, in life and in art.

The "gradual" in Stein's title does not refer to the time it took her to write the thousand-page narrative; rather it refers to the subjective accumulation of knowledge of herself and of others. As a young woman, she was interested in how people revealed themselves to others. This concern had initially a diagnostic dimension; if she knew intimately what motivated individuals (or herself) she might help change harmful behavior. In college this study of others took an inward turn and led her to William James and psychology. During an experiment to compare the differences between students in a normal state of activity with those suffering from exam-produced fatigue, Stein became fascinated by what she termed the "bottom nature" of individuals. This quality revealed itself through speech; the content of such discourse was less important than the features of repetition and cadence. Through a simple but faithful representation of these features, Stein felt it possible to describe every type of individual that ever had, did, or would exist (135–142). Years later however, the author was faced with two problems. She wanted to represent the totality of the individual as she experienced him/her. She also wanted to express that knowledge that had come about gradually but that she then apprehended instantaneously: "a great deal of The Making of Americans was a struggle to . . . make a whole present of something that . . . had taken a great deal of time to find out, but it was whole then and there within me and as such it had to be said" (147). The problem of expressing simultaneously gradual and immediate could in part be resolved by using the present participle. For Stein, it conveyed that "strictly American" ability: "to conceive a space that is filled with moving" (161).

Stein stumbled onto another solution to the problem of representing the temporal, in the patterns of colloquial speech. She became attentive to these patterns, when at age seventeen she moved from an isolated and introspective life in California to Baltimore, where she lived with "a whole group of very lively little aunts who had to know everything" (168). The aunts needing to know everything led to the telling and retelling of stories. No matter how many times a story was told, it was never repeated in the same way: "there can be no repetition because the essence of repetition is insistence, and if you insist you must each time use emphasis and if you use emphasis it is not possible while anybody is alive that they . . . use exactly the same emphasis" (167). Just as people reveal their "bottom nature" through repetition with subtle variation, Stein believed an analogous literary form could reveal the innate and immediate vitality of her subject. Stein began this effort in *The Making of Americans,* but it did not come to fruition until she began writing portraits.

Stein realized that "insistence" alone would not convey the "immediate existing" of her subject. There remained the challenge of extricating from a portrait any trace of her memory of the subject. Memory, we recall from *Everybody's Autobiography,* interfered with creativity. Truly creative work was accomplished when the artist apprehended the subject by simultaneously "listening" and "talking," as Steiner put it, "perfect merging of action and response, stimulus and affect" (xix). For example, Stein offers: "We in this period have not lived in remembering, we have living in moving" (181). The first verb, "have lived," is in the present perfect, highlighting its definitiveness, and its negation, "not," emphasizes the point. The second verb, "have," completed with "living" is Stein's use of the present participle to push to its grammatical limits the fact of its present-ness. Now consider this version: "We in this period live not in remembering, we live in movement." This configuration is grammat-ically more conventional, but it does not convey with the same force, the quality of present movement. The truly "exciting thing inside anyone . . . is not a remembered thing . . . it is not a repeated thing" (183). Nor is it a conventional thing.

Stein notes a parallel to the expression of immediacy through rep-etition with subtle variation (which did not depend on memory) in the motion picture: "Funnily enough the cinema has offered a solu-tion to this thing. By a continuously moving picture of any one there is no memory of any other thing and there is that thing existing, it is in a way . . . one portrait of anything not a number of them" (176). She attributes the similarity between her writing and the motion pic-ture to the era in which she lived, "any one is of one's period and this our period was undoubtedly the period of the cinema and series pro-duction . . . each of us in our own way are bound to express what the world in which we are living is doing" (177). The movies and series production, like Stein herself, are phenomena of the modern Ameri-can times.

Interestingly, one of Stein's teachers at Radcliffe was Hugo Mün-sterberg, who in 1916 published a study on this very novel form: *The Photoplay: A Psychological Study.* Münsterberg observes that "the motion pictures are lifted above the world of space and time and causality and are freed from its bounds" (185). But he goes on to argue that despite this freedom, motion pictures must adhere to the Aristotelian unities of action and character. Stein may have read *The Photoplay,* but it is clear that she did not share her professor's conclusions.

At the First Congress of Negro Artists and Writers, Richard Wright, Léopold Senghor, Aimé Césaire, Cedric Dover, and scholars and artists from twenty-four nations representing the whole of the African Diaspora took up the problem of novel aesthetic and social forms. The congress convened in Paris in September 1956 under the auspices of the French journal, *Présence Africaine*. In fact, James Baldwin covered the congress in an essay, "Princes and Powers." It was the first gathering of its kind, and Wright played an active role in its organization; he was the liaison between members of the delegation and those representing the United States. The members of the American delegation were Horace Mann Bond, Mercer Cook, John A. Davis, William Fontaine, and James Ivy (Fabre, *Unfinished* 435).

There are two versions of Wright's lecture for this event: the one he prepared for the Congress, "Tradition and Industrialization: The Plight of the Tragic Elite in Africa," which appears in the special edition of *Présence Africaine*, and "Tradition and Industrialization: The Historic Meaning of the Plight of the Tragic Elite in Africa and Asia," which was published in *White Man Listen!* The differences between these versions illuminate Wright's awareness of the two very different audiences and an attention to their separate concerns. For example, one important difference between the opening remarks of the text in *Présence Africaine* and those in *White Man, Listen!* is the absence in the former of any reference to Wright's past membership in the American Communist Party. Wright had to include this disclaimer for his American readership, who, in the context of McCarthyism, would dismiss his comments because of that affiliation. But in Paris many of the delegates to the congress were communists, including Aimé Césaire. Wright did not want to alienate such people, even though he no longer believed in the efficacy of communism. Similarly Wright excludes the attack on the Catholic Church (84–85) from the *Présence Africaine* lecture; there were Catholics present at the congress, notably Léopold Senghor.

Indeed when *White Man, Listen!* appeared, Senghor took exception to Wright's criticism of the Catholic Church in a July 21, 1959, letter to him. After congratulating him on his courage for telling "a few healthy truths" to both whites and blacks, Senghor added, "I'll make one reservation only. You cannot hide your distrust of Christianity in general and Roman Catholicism in particular. I can easily account for this distrust through your situation as an American Negro, as a man of Anglo-Saxon and Protestant culture. I do not think, however, that this distrust is well-founded. The facts prove

that the Catholic Church has pursued . . . a strong effort towards
de colonization. To such a point that a colonist was able to call one of
his books *Vatican Against France*. Of course, I am myself a Catholic
of Latin culture, which may render me partial. Yet I believe that I
am clear sighted enough for my partiality not to be exaggerated"
(Ray 149).

For *White Man, Listen!* Wright included material he could not
have judiciously used in the lecture to the congress. For example:

> I shiver when I learn that the infant mortality rate . . . in James Town . . .
> is fifty percent in the first year of life . . . I'm speechless when I learn that
> this inhuman condition is explained by the statement, "The children did
> not wish to stay. Their ghostmothers called them home." I know that there
> can be no altering of social conditions in those areas until such religious
> rationalizations have been swept from men's minds. . . . I can conceive of
> no identification with such mystical visions of life . . . no matter how emo-
> tionally satisfying such degradation seems to those who wallow in it. (80)

(Interestingly Nina Kressner Cobb mistakenly assumed that this
passage was included in Wright's address to the congress because
she did not consult the special edition of *Présence Africaine* that
reprinted every speech presented at the congress [235]. Wright
scholarship too often suffers from inaccuracy, but this error also encourages Wright's exaggerated reputation as a loose cannon. Wright
disapproved of much of what he had seen in Africa, and he voiced
his opinion, but he was neither insensitive nor tactless.)

In both versions of the lecture, Wright accuses Christianity of endorsing Western racism, but he credits the Protestant Reformation
for creating a society in which the Enlightenment and secular hu-
manist values could flourish.

The delegates to the congress were obliged to confine their remarks to issues of artistic expression. George Lamming and Léopold
Senghor cited Wright's work as an example of an essentially African
artistic sensibility. Léopold Senghor argued that *Black Boy* as well
as some of Wright's early poetry resembled "Negro-African" literature. Cedric Dover invoked Wright's "Blueprint for Negro Writing,"

as he argued for a cultural nationalism for black literature. And George Lamming compared Amos Tutuola's *Palm Wine Drunkard* and Roger Mais's *Brother Man* to Wright's *Black Boy* (Fabre, *Unfinished* 435–37). But important differences in worldviews quickly emerged: as Léopold Senghor extolled the wealth and beauty of African poetry, Wright questioned the serviceability of the traditional religious beliefs from which that poetry had sprung. Only Aimé Césaire addressed the relationship between colonization and culture that corresponded to Wright's concerns.

Césaire's argument echoes much of what Wright had touched on in *Black Power* and *The Color Curtain*. Césaire stated:

> Wherever colonialization is a fact the indigenous culture begins to rot. And, among these ruins, something begins to be born which is not a culture but a kind of subculture, a subculture which is condemned to exist on the margin allowed it by European culture. This then becomes the province of a few men, the elite, who find themselves placed in the most artificial conditions, deprived of any revivifying contact with the masses of people. Under such conditions, this subculture has no chance whatever of growing into an active living culture. (203)

The emergence of a new African culture, a synthesis of both traditional and modern elements, could only be achieved through political and economic independence. For without such independence, the emerging culture would be severed from its roots: "I refuse to believe that a future African culture would be able to oppose a complete and brutal rejection of the ancient African culture" (204). The elite must prepare the way for those who will determine the forms and features of this new culture: the African people. Wright approved of Césaire's focus on the role of colonialism in the transformation of traditional African societies. But Césaire applauded aspects of those societies: the art of African sculpture, the democratic village, tribal solidarity, and a philosophy founded on a respect for life and the integrity of the cosmos, whereas Wright was unable to fit any feature of tribal life into a portrait of a modern state. Again, the problem is temporal; does one prepare for modern warfare with fencing lessons? For Césaire, the problem is only incidentally temporal; his major concern is the continued presence of Europe in Africa's economic and political life. The old culture may be rotting, but there is a new culture, a vital syncretic mélange, waiting to emerge.

Before beginning his address to the congress, Wright noted with regret the paucity of women in attendance: "In our struggle for freedom, against great odds, we cannot afford to ignore one half of our manpower, that is the force of women. . . . Black men will not be free until their women are free" (348). Even though "manpower" and the possessive pronoun "their" betrays him, he was the only delegate to recognize the absence of women. Wright's address to the congress begins with a response to Cedric Dover's use of "Blueprint for Negro Writing" to argue for cultural nationalism. Wright notes that when he wrote the essay in 1937 the situation between black and white Americans was much more hostile than in 1956. But recent changes in the United States, namely the Supreme Court's ruling on *Brown v. the Board of Education,* gave him reason to hope: "If these implementations of American law continue, and as they continue, that nationalism of itself will be liquidated. I hope that even though I wrote those lines to justify Black Nationalism in America, that they need not remain valid for decades to come" (347). Wright observes that the comparison of the situation of black Americans with that of the Africans is imperfect. Indeed, much of what he had learned from the other delegates had forced him to change some of his opinions. Rather than rewrite his paper (and miss the other talks) he amended it as he went along.

As in the introduction to *White Man, Listen!* Wright insists on the subjectivity of his remarks. He first establishes his position as a Western man of color and underlines his divided allegiance. Echoing Du Bois's famous formulation: "This double vision of mine stems from my being a product of Western civilization and from my racial identity . . . Being a Negro living in a white Western Christian society, I've never been allowed to blend, in a natural healthy manner, with the culture and civilization of the West. This contradiction . . . creates a distance . . . between me and my environment . . . Hence though Western, I'm inevitably critical of the West" (349). Still, he emphasizes those features of Western culture he most admires: the separation of church and state, individual right to free thought and speech, the autonomy of artistic expression and scientific inquiry. Wright stresses the absence of metaphysics in his worldview; this is the significant difference between him and the majority of the delegates. Wright's understanding of the colonial and postcolonial world illustrates this difference.

In their effort to conquer the colored peoples of the world, Western nations had sown in their hearts the seeds of discontent and eventual revolution. Wright suggests that the former subject peoples owed the white man a debt of gratitude; "Thank you, Mr. White Man for freeing me from the rot of my irrational traditions and customs, though you are still the victim of your own irrational customs and traditions" (355). But in the first of several parenthetical remarks, Wright admits: "I wrote this paper up in the country, projecting an ideal room filled with secular minded Africans more or less like myself . . . Being an American Negro with but few lingering vestiges of my irrational heritage in *both* America and Africa, I felt I could be detached. But I place a question mark, in public, behind that statement" (355). Does the question mark modify his ability to be detached or does it apply to the entire quotation? Wright then claims that the elite of the former colonies were the most secular-minded people in the world. But after a delegate from the clergy argued that Africans were "incurably religious," Wright again pauses to question his own assertion. And when he claims that Western ravages of the traditional societies had created the conditions in which truly democratic societies could fill the void, he stops again to wonder. Wright concludes that the elite of Africa and Asia are the "FREEST MEN IN ALL THE WORLD TODAY," but then adds that perhaps all of his assertions are more ideal than real (356). Wright's inability to speak for the Africans, whose political and economic independence had dominated his energies and imagination for over a decade, measures the deep-seated historical and cultural differences between Africans and African Americans. Although these groups shared the experience of white oppression, African Americans, like European

Americans, created and were created by modernity, which is the American experience.

Richard Wright's intellectual and creative energy developed in a lifelong effort to understand if not redeem the African Diaspora. Wright saw this event as the single most important component in the making of modernity; and subsequently he would argue that the Diaspora made black folk the first moderns. On the dust jacket of *Pagan Spain*, he stated: "The white man had unknowingly freed me of my traditional, backward culture, but had clung fiercely to his own" (Fabre, *Richard Wright Reader* 110–11). Through the Middle Passage and chattel slavery, black Americans had come in contact with those Western values Wright most admired, but his statement reveals the extent to which he believed that most Westerners had yet to accept, in their hearts and minds, the principles upon which their civilization was founded. Richard Wright, the son of a sharecropper and descendant of slaves, believed his claim to an American identity was greater because his freedom, civil rights, and citizenship had been won at such high costs.

Conclusion

In their explorations of place and displacement, of home and origins, of poetics and politics, Gertrude Stein and Richard Wright call for new narratives. In *Paris France, Everybody's Autobiography,* and *Lectures in America,* Gertrude Stein foregrounds her most important contributions to American modernism and more. Stein's emphasis on radical subjectivity and her experiments with temporal representation argue the impossibility of the definitive in life or art. These innovations place contingency and indeterminacy at the center of the experience of modernity and, by extension, modernist poetics. Stein's linguistic innovations depend on distance: the physical distance between Oakland and New York, France and the United States, the psychological distance between black and white Americans, Americans and Europeans, between the nineteenth and twentieth centuries. This distance underscored the modernist's sense of rupture, discontinuity, and the need for new forms of expression. Stein had to abandon the stasis of the noun for the activity of verbs and the indeterminacy of prepositions; she rejected the symmetry of beginning, middle, and end for the asymmetry of beginning a text with Chapter VI because "there is no reason why chapters should succeed each other since nothing succeeds another, not now any more" (*Geographical* 90).

Looking back, Stein argues that the features of her writing were an expression of an American ethos, where American becomes synonymous with modernity. It was everywhere apparent: in language, architecture, air travel; even the landscape mirrored modernist painting in its abstract qualities. Stein's poetics also point to the key observation that America is a creole culture and American modernism emerges in the context of an urban, heterogeneous society. That which was truly American, from the experience of time to patterns of speech, developed, as she reminded her Ivy League audiences, through an extended, usually antagonistic encounter with the Other. Just as Stein found her voice by donning the mask of an African American, so too did American art, music, speech, and architecture embody that dialectical relationship. The poetics of American modernism did not develop in creative writing classes at Harvard; they emerged, as Michael North argues, from the volatile mix of so-called standard English and the urban dialects of African Americans and European immigrants (3–34). The mimetic alienation characteristic of Stein's poetics highlights the rupture, displacement, and dissonance of alien accents, which rendered the familiar quite strange and quite new. Stein's poetics confirmed Richard Wright's challenge to the social and political status quo. They also encouraged Wright's need for distance from the subject matter of his art.

Richard Wright journeys to Spain and Africa to discover the origins of the modern world and, by extension, his own as well. But he has also come to bear witness at the crossroads of the postwar period. It was an extraordinary moment; centuries of European colonialism in Africa and Asia were at an end, and the former colonies would emerge new nations. The world's maps would be redrawn and nations' names would change to mark the new world order. In this context, the journeys Wright narrates in *Pagan Spain* and *Black Power* and the lectures in *White Man, Listen!* develop and expand his larger thesis: to understand modernity (of which postcolonialism is another chapter) one must understand Africa and the African American's role in its making. At midcentury, Wright pauses to ask: How did the Africans become slaves? What was the impact of slavery on those who survived the Middle Passage? What was the impact of slavery on white Europeans and Americans? Furthering Du Bois's "Would America have been America without her Negro People?" Wright contends that "the Negro is America's metaphor." That is, much like Stein's artist whose genius is nurtured through a dialectical relationship between the margin (geographic, gender, ethnic, racial) and the center (heterosexuality, ethnic and/or racial majorities) the "Negro" is quintessentially American: his/her history and blood are figuratively and literally inextricably bound up with that of his/her white American peers.

In *Pagan Spain* and *Black Power*, Wright assumes the sometimes naive travel writer's persona to narrate his encounter with the African American's past. Just as Washington Irving, Gertrude Stein, and Ernest Hemingway claim Spain as the site of America's origins, so too does America's native son. Wright later recalled that the journey to Spain made clear to him the extent to which he was a child of the West but more important a child of modernity. Wright's encounter with this Catholic nation illustrated the chasm between himself and the descendants of the Spanish Empire. Wright's journey to Africa is a return to the ancestral homeland and a confirmation of his distance from those ancestors and that homeland. In these narratives, the terms "origins" and "home" must be read ironically; at the very least they must acknowledge the contingency and indeterminacy of American identity, of which the notion of origins is a part. *Pagan Spain* and *Black Power* emphasize the creole aspect of Spanish culture and point to evidence of West African influence on African-American cultural forms. In this way, Wright draws attention to the creole quality of American culture and the impossibility of investing in the idea of "racial" or "cultural" purity. America could not locate the origin of its body politic in any one place. Nor, Wright went on to argue, should African Americans subscribe to the distorted view of themselves and their role in the making of the modern world, a view that had been fashioned by centuries of racist theory and practice. In his last works of literature, Wright explores the aesthetic implications of this position.

In "Five Episodes from an Unfinished Novel," published posthumously, Wright places the protagonist from his last completed novel, *The Long Dream,* in Paris. Fishbelly Tucker boards a plane for Paris because his high-school buddies are now GIs stationed there and because it is far from Mississippi, from which he has barely escaped with his life. These vignettes describe Fish's early days in Paris, where he encounters an alien French world (where Africans walk hand in hand with willowy blondes) as well as the strange world of black expatriates. In his early encounters with the concierge and the *patronne* of the restaurant, Fish is less struck by the foreignness of the French or their customs than by his responses to them. That the extent of his French is *oui* and *merci* is not an obstacle. Wright sprinkles the stories with French, from the simple "quel chapeau americain" to the more grammatically complex "Je regrette que vous ayez été tellement derangé."

But innocent, even playful gestures become heart-stopping episodes because Fish assumes that the French are motivated by the same racism as white Americans. In one vignette, Fishbelly, dressed like a hipster, ventures onto the scene of an anti-NATO demonstration. The students, seeing Fish's stunning hat, decide to take it from him and give chase. Fishbelly assumes they want to lynch him and flies back to his hotel. But the mob follows him there chanting all the while, "quel chapeau americain." Mme Couteau, the owner/concierge, protects her client by surrendering his hat. The mob cheers and disperses (143–45). This point is made again in another story where Fishbelly assumes that a woman refuses to give up her table at a restaurant because she is racist. In fact, she has misplaced her teeth and understandably does not want to leave without them (148). Unlike Ned, the Wright-figure of these stories, the other black expatriates, Irene, Jimmy, and Woodie, have been so traumatized by American racism that the alternative culture does not provide them with other ways of seeing black/white relations. Irene and Jimmy are the hustlers they were back in the States, "steaming" white folks of as much money as possible. Woodie, a brilliant law student gone mad, believes that white people are trying to control the solar system by decreasing the force of gravity. Through these pieces, set in a foreign context, Wright focuses on the provincialism of black Americans (not unlike that of white Americans) and criticizes American racism, which, in these characters, has made that provincialism pathological.

Richard Wright left the United States and lies buried in Paris's Père Lachaise cemetery, (a three minute walk from Stein's grave) in part for the freedom to write what most interested him. At the end of his too brief life, he wrote haiku. That a volume of Wright's haiku has yet to appear in print further makes this point; in America black boys do not write haiku. But in the last year of his life, Richard Wright wrote thousands of the seventeen-syllable poems. A small number of the haiku were chosen for *The Richard Wright Reader.* Some evoke a physical and psychic peace: "I would like a bell / Toiling in this soft twilight / Over willow trees" and "Winter rain at night / Sweetening the taste of bread / And spicing the soup." Others are vivid photographs: "The green cockleburs / Caught in the thick woolly hair / Of the black boy's head" and "In the falling snow / A laughing boy holds out his palms / Until they are white." And still others suggest a somber mood: "I am nobody / A red sinking autumn sun / Took my name away" and finally "It is September / The month when I was born / And I have no thoughts" (251–54). Wright's achievement is more than aesthetic; writing haiku, apparently antithetical to the American ethos in its spareness and rigid formality, suggests the extent to which Wright embraced and furthered the heterogeneity of American literature and the America aesthetic.

In *Brewsie and Willie,* the last work of fiction to be published in her lifetime, Stein responds to Wright's request that she return to the States for a lecture tour. Set in postwar France, *Brewsie and Willie* records the concerns of American GIs as they prepare to return home. The war and the experience of French and German cultures call into question American social, political, and economic systems. Brewsie, the Steinian figure and the "outfit's thinker" provokes the soldiers and Red Cross nurses to question the continued viability of capitalism, industrialization, and a consumer economy. Brewsie and the nurses also raise the problem of civil rights for women and African Americans. The formal qualities of the text are prototypical Gertrude Stein, but the content owes much to Richard Wright. Wright read *Brewsie and Willie* in galleys and reviewed it for *PM Magazine,* and his influence on the text is apparent.

Brewsie and Willie couples Socratic Brewsie with his foil Willie.

Willie, like the echo of his name, is both willful and willing. His willfulness is redeemed only by his willingness to listen to Brewsie. The text is an ongoing conversation between several GIs and Red Cross nurses that replicates informal discussion. And although some characters share similar views, no two are identical. The formal characteristics of *Brewsie and Willie* underscore its central theme: the well-being of the nation depended on thinking individuals challenging the fundamental tenets of American life. The problems raised are never resolved, but again, as is typical of Stein, the emphasis is on the process of inquiry. Like Socrates, Brewsie prompts a symposium that takes as its topic the future of the American enterprise, at the heart of which is the problem of American racism. Echoing Wright's observation that the Negro is America's metaphor, *Brewsie and Willie* uses the black American experience to highlight the evil and error of the American past and to point to hope for its future.

Early in the narrative, Brewsie and the GIs are discussing the possibility of another war. In response, GI Brock reports an exchange with a black major. The officer admitted that even though he had been married nine years, he had no children. When asked why, the major replies, "Is this America any place to make born a Negro child" (12). The major's response to American racism is to deny it another victim. But this anecdote also draws a parallel between the consequences of the racism of Nazi Germany and the systemic racism back home. This is further suggested in a piece Stein wrote for the *New York Times*. In this account of her meetings with the GIs, Stein simultaneously criticizes American racism and is hopeful that it will end: "A good many of the boys begin to know what the words imprisoned and persecution mean, when they see the millions . . . imprisoned for years persecuted for years, they begin to realize what minorities in a country are bound to lead to, to persecution and to a sense of imprisonment. When these American boys see all the instability of a . . . continent imprisoned as the whole of Europe has been . . . well . . . it does something to them, of course it does" ("New Hope" 38). Amidst the ruins of postwar Europe, Stein's critique of

Germany is vehement, but these attacks are carom shots aimed at the United States as well.

In June 1945, Stein and Toklas flew to Germany to visit the troops. *Life* magazine published her account of that visit, "Off We All Went to See Germany." They were the first American civilians to visit the soldiers, and although Stein faithfully records the grim evidence of war, her tone is cheerful. There is a particularly bright moment when she and the troops visit the Berchtesgaden, Hitler's country retreat. Stein and Toklas were photographed with the soldiers mocking the dictator's salute: "there we were in that big window where Hitler had dominated the world a bunch of GIs just gay and happy" (57). At the end of the four-day tour a sergeant handed her a card inscribed, "To Gertie, another Radical." Stein had earned this epithet because, like her character Brewsie, she engaged the GIs in lively debate. When they admitted that they liked the Germans better than other Europeans, she was furious: "Of course you do, . . . they flatter you and obey you when other countries don't like you and say so, and personally you have not been awfully ready to meet them halfway, well naturally if they don't like you they show it, the Germans don't like you but they flatter you . . . I bet you Fourth of July they will be putting up our flag, and all you big babies will be flattered to death, literally to death" (58).

This sentiment is echoed and extended in *Brewsie and Willie.* Now the GIs' attraction to Germany is indicative of something more disturbing. Brewsie asks, "do we like Germans because we are greedy and callous like them" (20). And afraid that he might weep, Brewsie asks the men to leave him before anyone replies. Similarly, GI Donald Paul draws the parallel between the United States and Germany, for despite appearances, Americans are, like the Germans, "old-fashioned." "We like 'em the Heinies, because they have electric lights . . . if there is anything old-fashioned it's that. . . . We think war is wine women and song and heroes, we're just old-fashioned, we believe in industrialism which makes us poor, we are just bloody old-fashioned" (50). Stein's criticism of German society becomes by association a searing critique of America. For even as she celebrated the young soldiers, she saw the bitter irony in the fact that the American army was a Jim Crow army. This ugly fact is documented in a photo of her among a group of African-American enlisted men (Stendhal 248–49).

In *Brewsie and Willie* the black solider serves as a measure of his white counterpart's provincialism and bigotry. Stein upends the notion that racism is limited to the South; her most bigoted soldiers are from "way up North." Interestingly, however, the black soldier is never a victim. En route to a bar, the GIs notice three black soldiers. One pauses before a woman and her young daughter. Cavalierlike, he goes down on one knee before the child and takes her hand. He speaks to her in French, then rises and walks on. Willie finds it odd that black soldiers always manage to speak French. And that he refers to the soldiers as "niggers" makes two points: Willie is a narrow-minded bigot, which impedes his ability to learn another language; so when he uses the word "nigger" to describe soldiers who are, from this gesture, not narrow-minded bigots, the term calibrates the limits of his imagination, experience, and compassion. Later Willie reports having seen a black soldier sharing a park bench with three white women. He then asks whether this for him aberrant behavior makes anyone else angry. Jo replies that although many of the GIs attempt to maintain a Jim Crow army, most of them don't care. The war put black and white Americans in such close proximity that they simply "can't feel mad about it" (42). Brewsie then asks, "when we get home will we get mad and all excited up about something that really doesn't amount to anything to us like we did before this war" (43).

Toward the end of the narrative when the GIs insist that he hold out some hope for their future, Brewsie says that they must return home and pioneer. And while Brewsie is still uncertain about what that means, Jimmie, the southerner, offers an example: "Yeah it's funny . . . the only real pioneering there is in America these days is done by Negroes. They're pioneering, they find new places, new homes, new lives, and they more and more own something, funny . . . kind of queer and funny" (65). This statement coincides with Stein's assessment of black Americans in *Everybody's Autobiography*, who, because of their marginal position in American society, are capable of the "genius" she believed necessary to any creative activity (279).

Of Gertrude Stein, Richard Wright wrote: "Perhaps more than any other mind of our time, she has realized acutely the difference between Yesterday and Today, the difference between living in a feudal society and in a modern industrialized one. And she has realized the difference that difference makes in the personalities of men and women" (*PM* 15–16). Of Wright Stein wrote, "when one Negro can write as Richard Wright does writing as a Negro about Negroes writes not as a Negro but as a man, well the minute that happens the relation between the white and the Negro is no longer a difference of races but a minority question and ends . . . in persecution" ("New Hope" 15, 38). Their separate journeys make visible their shared literary and cultural values and vision. And their efforts to understand and articulate the epistemological crisis of the twentieth century are the early maps of our postmodern world. Through their own peripatetic narratives, Gertrude Stein and Richard Wright bring light to our journey, and they wish us farewell.

Works Cited

Abrahams, Peter. "The Blacks." *An African Treasury: Articles, Essays, Stories by Black Africans.* Ed. Langston Hughes. New York: Crown Publishers, 1960.

Appiah, K. Anthony. "A Long Way From Home: Wright in the Gold Coast." *Richard Wright.* Ed. Harold Bloom. New York: Chelsea House, 1987.

Baker, Houston. *Modernism and the Harlem Renaissance.* Chicago: University of Chicago Press, 1987.

Baldwin, James. "Princes and Powers." *Nobody Knows My Name: More Notes of a Native Son.* New York: Dial, 1961.

Baraka, Amiri. "Notes For A Speech." *The Leroi Jones/Amiri Baraka Reader.* Ed. William Harris. New York: Thunder's Mouth Press, 1991.

Benjamin, Walter. *Illuminations: Essays and Reflections.* New York: Harcourt, Brace and World, 1968.

Benstock, Sheri. *Women of the Left Bank: Paris, 1900–1940.* Austin: University of Texas Press, 1986.

Blackmer, Corinne. "African Masks and the Arts of Passing in Gertrude Stein's 'Melanctha' and Nella Larsen's *Passing.*" *Journal of the History of Sexuality* 4.2 (1993): 230–63.

Bolland, O. Nigel. "Mannoni and Fanon: The Psychology of Colonization and the Decolonization of the Personality." *New Scholar* 4.1 (1973): 29–50.

Bridgman, Richard. *Gertrude Stein in Pieces.* New York: Oxford University Press, 1970.

Brinnin, John Malcolm. *The Third Rose: Gertrude Stein and Her World.* Reading, Mass.: Addison-Wesley, 1987.

Burns, Edward. *Gertrude Stein on Picasso.* New York: Liveright, 1970.

———, ed. *The Letters of Gertrude Stein and Carl Van Vechten, 1913–1946.* New Haven: Yale University Press, 1986.

Burns, Edward, and Ulla Dydo, eds. *The Letters of Gertrude Stein and Thornton Wilder.* New York: Columbia University Press, 1996.

Cappetti, Carla. *"Black Boy . . . Who Lived Underground*: Richard Wright Beyond Realism and Aestheticism." Paper delivered at Black Boy at Fifty Conference, Washington University, November 18, 1995.

———. *Writing Chicago: Modernism, Ethnography, and the Novel.* New York: Columbia University Press, 1993.

Castro, Americo. *The Structure of Spanish History.* Trans. Edmund King. New Jersey: Princeton University Press, 1954.

Césaire, Aimé. "Culture et colonisation." *Présence Africaine* 8–10 (1956): 190–205.

Cobb, Nina Kressner. "Richard Wright and the Third World." *Critical Essays on Richard Wright.* Ed. Yoshinobu Hakutani. Boston: G. K. Hall, 1982.

Danquah, J. B. *The Akan Doctrine of God.* London: Lutterworth, 1944.

DeKoven, Marianne. *A Different Language.* Madison: University of Wisconsin Press, 1983.

Devereux, George, and Edwin Loeb. "Antagonistic Acculturation." *American Sociological Review* 8.2 (1943): 133–47.

———. "Ethnic Identity: Its Logical Foundation and Its Dysfunctions." *Ethnic Identity: Cultural Continuities and Change.* Ed. George De Vos and Lola Ramanucci-Ross. Palo Alto: Mayfield, 1975.

Drake, St. Clair, and Horace Cayton. *Black Metropolis: A Study of Negro Life in a Northern City.* New York: Harcourt Brace, 1945.

Fabre, Michel. *Richard Wright: Books and Writers.* Jackson: University Press of Mississippi, 1990.

———. *The Unfinished Quest of Richard Wright.* Trans. Isabel Barzun. New York: Morrow, 1971.

———. *The World of Richard Wright.* Jackson: University Press of Mississippi, 1985.

Fabre, Michel, and Ellen Wright, eds. *Richard Wright Reader.* New York: Harper and Row, 1978.

Fanon, Frantz. *Black Skin, White Masks.* 1952. Trans. Charles Lam Markmann. New York: Grove Weidenfeld, 1967.

Faÿ, Bernard. *Les Précieux.* Paris: Librarie Académique Perrin, 1966.

Fifer, Elizabeth. "Is Flesh Advisable? The Interior Theater of Gertrude Stein." *Signs* 4 (1979): 472–83.

———. *Rescued Readings: A Reconstruction of Stein's Difficult Texts.* Detroit: Wayne State University Press, 1992.

Fineman, Joel. "The History of the Anecdote: Fiction and Fiction." *The New Historicism.* Ed. H. Aram Veeser. New York: Routledge, 1988.

Fischer, Louis. *Gandhi: His Life and Message for the World.* New York: Signet, 1954.

Gassner, John. Introduction. *Aristotle's Theory of Poetry and Fine Art.* By S. H. Butcher. 1894. New York: St. Martin's, 1951.

Gibbs, Anna. "Hélène Cixous and Gertrude Stein: New Directions in Feminist Criticism." *Meanjin* 38 (1979): 281–93.

Gilroy, Paul. *The Black Atlantic: Modernity and Double Consciousness.* Cambridge: Harvard University Press, 1993.

———. *Small Acts: Thoughts on the Politics of Black Cultures.* London: Serpent's Tail, 1993.

Greenblatt, Stephen. *Learning to Curse: Essays in Early Modern Culture.* New York: Routledge, 1990.

———. *Marvelous Possessions: The Wonder of the New World.* Chicago: University of Chicago Press, 1991.

Haas, Robert, ed. *A Primer for the Gradual Understanding of Gertrude Stein.* Los Angeles: Black Sparrow Press, 1971.

Hemingway, Ernest. *The Sun Also Rises.* New York: Scribner and Sons, 1926.

Herrnstein, Richard. *Bell Curve: Intelligence and Class Structure in American Life.* New York: Free Press, 1994.

Hollinger, David. "The Knower and the Artificer." *American Quarterly* 39 (1987): 37–55.

Hooker James R. *Black Revolutionary: George Padmore's Path from Communism to Pan-Africanism.* London: Praeger, 1967.

Hughes, Langston. *The Ways of White Folks.* 1934. New York: Vintage, 1971.

Hulme, Peter. *Colonial Encounters: Europe and the Native Caribbean, 1492–1797.* London: Routledge, 1986.

Irving, Washington. *The Alhambra.* New York: G. P. Putnam, 1851.

Johnson, Charles. *Oxherding Tale.* New York: Grove Press, 1982.

Jung, Carl. "Your Negroid and Indian Behavior." *Forum* 83.5 (1930): 193–99.

Kent, Raymond. *From Madagascar to the Malagasy Republic.* New York: Praeger, 1962.

Mannoni, Octave. *Psychologie de la Colonisation.* Paris: Seuil, 1950.

———. *Prospero and Caliban.* Trans. Pamela Powesland. New York: Praeger, 1956.

Margolies, Edward. *The Art of Richard Wright.* Carbondale: Southern Illinois University Press, 1969.

Mellow, James. *Charmed Circle: Gertrude Stein and Company.* Boston: Houghton Mifflin, 1974.

Miller, Eugene. *The Voice of a Native Son: The Poetics of Richard Wright.* Jackson: University Press of Mississippi, 1990.

Münsterberg, Hugo. *The Photoplay: A Psychological Study.* New York: Appleton and Company, 1916.

Murray, Albert. *The Omni Americans.* 1970. New York: Random House, 1983.

Neuman, Shirley Swartz. *Gertrude Stein and the Problem of Narration.* British Columbia: English Literary Studies, 1979.

Nkrumah, Kwame. *Dark Days in Ghana.* London: Lawrence and Wishart, 1968.

North, Michael. *The Dialect of Modernism: Race, Language, and Twentieth Century Literature.* New York: Oxford University Press, 1994.

Olivan, Federico. "A propósito de 'La España Pagana': el negro que tení el alma negra inspira una versión grotesca de la opera 'Carmen.' " Review of *Pagan Spain,* by Richard Wright. *A Richard Wright Bibliography: Fifty Years of Criticism and Commentary, 1933–1982.* Ed. Keneth Kinnamon. New York: Greenwood Press, 1988.

Ottley, Roi. "He Should Stick to Fiction." Review of *Pagan Spain,* by Richard Wright. *Chicago Sun Tribune Magazine of Books* 3 Mar. 1957: 10.

Park, Robert. "Human Migration and the Marginal Man." *Race and Culture.* Ed. Everett C. Hughes. New York: Arno, 1974.

Patterson, Orlando. *Slavery and Social Death.* Cambridge: Harvard University Press, 1982.

Pratt, Mary Louise. *Imperial Eyes: Travel Writing and Transculturation.* New York: Routledge, 1992.

Rattray, Robert S. *Ashanti.* 1923. New York: Negro Universities Press, 1969.

Ray, David, and Robert Farnsworth, eds. *Richard Wright: Impressions and Perspectives.* Ann Arbor: University of Michigan Press, 1973.

Saunders, Judith. "Gertrude Stein's *Paris France* and the American Literary Tradition." *South Dakota Review* 1.15 (1977): 7–17.

Sollors, Werner. *Amiri Baraka/Leroi Jones: The Quest for a Populist Modernism.* New York: Columbia University Press, 1978.

———. *Beyond Ethnicity: Consent and Descent in American Culture.* New York: Oxford University Press, 1986.

Stein, Gertrude. *The Autobiography of Alice B. Toklas.* New York: Random House, 1933.

———. *Brewsie and Willie.* New York: Random House, 1946.

———. *Everybody's Autobiography.* New York: Random House, 1937.

———. "Film. Deux soeurs qui ne sont pas des soeurs." *Operas and Plays.* Paris: Plain Edition, 1932.

———. *Four Saints In Three Acts. Last Operas and Plays.* Ed. Carl Van Vechten. New York: Rinehart, 1949.

———. *The Geographical History of America, Or the Relation of Human Nature to the Human Mind.* New York: Random House, 1936.

———. *The Making of Americans.* 1925. New York: Something Else Press, 1966.

———. *Narration: Four Lectures by Gertrude Stein.* 1935. New York: Greenwood Press, 1969.

———. "The New Hope Is 'Our Sad Young Man.' " *New York Times Magazine* 3 June 1945: 15, 38.

———. "Off We All Went to See Germany." *Life* 6 Aug. 1945: 54–58.

———. *Paris France.* New York: Scribner's, 1940.

———. *Picasso.* London: B. T. Batsford, 1938.

———. *Things As They Are: A Novel in Three Parts.* Pawlet, Vt.: Banyan, 1950.

———. *What Are Masterpieces.* Los Angeles: Conference Press, 1940.

Stein, Leo. *A Journey into the Self.* Ed. Edmund Fuller. New York: Crown, 1950.

Steiner, Wendy. Introduction. *Lectures in America.* By Gertrude Stein. 1935. Boston: Beacon Press, 1985.

Stendhal, Renate, ed. *Gertrude Stein in Words and Pictures.* Chapel Hill, N.C.: Algonquin, 1994.

Tubbs, Vincent. "Gertrude Stein Talks for Afro." *Baltimore Afro-American* 28 July 1945: 5.

Van Vechten, Carl, ed. *Selected Writings of Gertrude Stein.* New York: Random House, 1946.

Wald, Pricilla. *Constituting Americans: Cultural Anxiety and Narrative Form.* Durham: Duke University Press, 1995.

Washington, Booker T. *Up from Slavery.* New York: Doubleday, 1901.

White, Walter. *Rope and Faggot: A Biography of Judge Lynch.* New York: Knopf, 1929.

Wirth, Louis. "Urbanism as a Way of Life." *On Cities and Social Life.* Ed. Albert J. Reiss. Chicago: University of Chicago Press, 1981.

Wright, Richard. "American GIs' Fears Worry Gertrude Stein." Review of *Brewsie and Willie,* by Gertrude Stein. *PM* 21 July 1946: 15–16.

———. *American Hunger.* New York: Harper and Row, 1977.

———. *Black Power: A Record of Reactions in a Land of Pathos.* New York: Harper's, 1954.

———. "Blueprint for Negro Writers." *Richard Wright Reader.* Ed. Michel Fabre and Ellen Wright. New York: Harper and Row, 1978.

———. *The Color Curtain: A Report on the Bandung Conference.* New York: World Publishing, 1956.

———. *Eight Men.* New York: Thunder's Mouth Press, 1987.

————. "Five Episodes from an Unfinished Novel." *Soon, One Morning: New Writing by American Negroes.* Ed. Herbert Hill. New York: Knopf, 1972.

————. "Gertrude Stein's Story is Drenched in Hitler's Horrors." Review of *Wars I Have Seen,* by Gertrude Stein. *PM* 11 Mar. 1945: 5.

————. "I Tried to Be a Communist." *The God That Failed.* Ed. Richard Crossman. New York: Harper's, 1949.

————. Journal typescript. James Weldon Johnson Collection, Beinecke Library, Yale University.

————. *Lawd Today!* 1960. *Richard Wright: Early Works.* New York: Library of America, 1991.

————. Letter to Gertrude Stein. 29 Oct. 1945. James Weldon Johnson Collection, Beinecke Library, Yale University.

————. "Littérature noire américaine." *Les Temps Modernes* 35 (Aug. 1948): 194–221.

————. "Memories of My Grandmother." Unpublished essay. James Weldon Johnson Collection. Beinecke Library, Yale University.

————. *Native Son.* New York: Harper's, 1940.

————. "The Neuroses of Conquest." Review of *Prospero and Caliban,* by Octave Mannoni. *Nation* 20 Oct. 1956: 330–31.

————. *Pagan Spain: A Report of a Journey into the Past.* New York: Harper's, 1957.

————. *Savage Holiday.* New York: Avon, 1953.

————. "Tradition and Industrialization: The Plight of the Tragic Elite in Africa." *Présence Africaine* 8–10 (1956): 347–60.

————. "Two American Negroes in Key Posts of Spain's Loyalist Forces." *Daily Worker* 19 Sept. 1937: 2.

————. "Walter Garland Tells What Spain's Fight Against Fascism Means to the Negro People." *Daily Worker* 29 Nov. 1937: 2.

————. *White Man, Listen!* New York: Harper's, 1957.

————. "Why I Chose 'Melanctha.'" *I Wish I'd Written That.* Ed. Whit Burnett. New York: McGraw Hill, 1946.

Index

World War II, 18–20, 40, 41, 43–45, 101, 133–37

Wright, Richard: acquaintance with Stein, 18, 20–21, 97, 133; aesthetics, 2, 8, 10, 11; in Africa, 24, 34, 42, 52, 57–63, 66–69, 72–81, 87–88, 90, 93–95, 102–04; background, 2, 5–6; and the Communist Party, 6–7; correspondence, 4, 5, 20–21, 31, 97; expatriation, 5, 17, 22–23, 27–28; first visit to France, 3; influence, 4, 11–12, 13–15, 18; journal entries, 4, 57–58; in Spain, 29–35; and Spanish Civil War, 41; on Stein, 3–4, 9, 16–17, 29, 40, 48, 119, 137; **Works:** *American Hunger*, 4, 5, 7, 14; "Between the World and Me," 118; *Black Boy*, 2, 5, 9, 14–15, 18, 20, 28, 42, 78, 90, 96, 123, 124; *Black Power*, 21, 23–24, 42, 51, 52, 57–63, 66–69, 72–81, 87–88, 90–92, 93–94, 101, 102, 112–13, 124, 130, 131; "Blueprint for Negro Writing," 8, 118, 123–24, 125; *The Color Curtain*, 42, 112, 124; "Five Episodes from an Unfinished Novel," 81, 131; haiku, 133; "I Tried to Be a Communist," 7; *Lawd Today!*, 4, 8–9, 79; "The Literature of the Negro in the United States," 115–19; *The Long Dream*, 81, 131–32; "The Man Who Lived Underground," 9–10; "Memories of My Grandmother," 15–16, 17; "The Miracle of Nationalism in the African Gold Coast," 102–04; *Native Son*, 2, 9, 22, 42, 52, 58, 79, 88, 89, 90–91, 92; *The Outsider*, 41; *Pagan Spain*, 22, 27, 28, 29–35, 39–40, 41, 48, 49–50, 60, 78, 101, 127, 130, 131; "The Psychological Reaction of Oppressed People," 107–12, 113; *The Richard Wright Reader*, 133; *Savage Holiday*, 41, 81; "Speech for a White Audience," 115–16; "Tarbaby's Dawn," 10–11; "Tradition and Industrialization," 119, 122–27; *Uncle Tom's Children*, 2, 21, 89; *White Man, Listen!*, 22, 24, 25, 78, 81, 97–98, 101–04, 107–13, 115–19, 122–27, 130

Zola, Emile, 11